THE GUTLESS
WONDER

THE GUTLESS WONDER

TOM ROONEY

authorHOUSE®

AuthorHouse™
1663 Liberty Drive
Bloomington, IN 47403
www.authorhouse.com
Phone: 1-800-839-8640

Published by AuthorHouse   04/10/2013

ISBN: 978-1-4817-3979-5 (sc)
ISBN: 978-1-4817-3976-4 (hc)
ISBN: 978-1-4817-3980-1 (e)

Library of Congress Control Number: 2013906559

CONTENTS

This book is dedicated with love and appreciation
to my lovely wife for her gracious and compassionate
caring to others; and to her friend Judy Thornton Stark,
who encouraged me to complete this work.

ACKNOWLEDGMENTS

A very small book was given to me while I was writing this story. The book was a favorite of Judy Thornton Stark, author and wife of Dr. Richard Boies Stark, noted artist and plastic surgeon. Reading Springs of Greek Wisdom, by Herder Book Center New York Copyright 1968 by Leobuchhandlung, I found the passages so appropriate for the introduction of each chapter. I hope you enjoy them as I did.

Jenny Hundertmark, a Lutheran School teacher spent tireless hours during a very serious illness and recovery to edit the book for grammar and punctuation. Thank you Jenny and for your comment of the chapter on the Last Run made you cry.

Thank you to my illustrator/graphic artist, Rey Flores. His effort and devotion to his art was greatly appreciated and added the right touch for the book.

Men are not worried by things, but by their ideas about thing.
When we meet with difficulties, become anxious or troubled,
Let us not blame others, but rather ourselves,
That is: our ideas about things.
Epictetus

CHAPTER 1

THE JUNIOR YEAR

The morning was overcast and gloomy. Not like other first days of school in September when the sun was out, everyone was smiling, new clothes for a fresh start, and happy attitudes. This was the beginning of the 1960's.

Tom Rooney got out of his mom's new car, a cool red and white 1957 Chevrolet. She stopped in front of the school, and all the kids' head were turning to look at the cool car. Tom and his mom were to share this car for the next couple of years. The car was purchased by his mother's new boyfriend for them to use.

Oakbrook High School still looked as new as it did three years ago when it opened. It was the newest architectural design, and it really appeared to be years ahead of anything built in the 60's. It was two stories tall, round with classrooms surrounding a gymnasium, and a balcony providing excellent view of all activities held there. A dome covered the center ceiling of the gym that gave excellent natural light and a great echo when bouncing a basketball or a cheer from cheerleaders that carried throughout the building.

Everyone wore their new school clothes, sporting the latest fads and of course the latest in hairstyles of the 60's. Girls were wearing bobby socks with white and black saddle oxfords. Girls from the middle class families could be identified by the new shoes as apposed to the less fortunate families who had newly polished oxfords or with a different style shoe. Guys were wearing the latest in young men' shoes that had soles at least ¾ to 1 inch thick, black, and laces the same color. The parents were sure the boys were going to be stooped shouldered from carrying around those heavy shoes. Belts were thin width and worn off center from the front of the jeans or slacks. Most boys wore blue jeans, cuffed at least once at the bottom, just touching the top of the shoes as to have no break in the crease.

The hairdos were a rage, to say the least, and one was cool by how many different parts were in the hair. Girls wore high beehive hairstyle held together with lots of hair spray. Tom sported what was called a Princeton; two parts on each side, combed to the center, then down to the front of his forehead, where two spit curls met to give the appearance of having it all under control. Oh yes, the sides and back had the trademark of an Elvis fan with the famous D.A.!

These hairdos brought about endless trips to the bathroom and required the use of a plastic comb to be protruding from the back pocket of your blue jeans. Strict attention was paid to the slightest hair out of place and dashes in and out of the bathroom just before and after each bell to change classes was the order of the day.

Strange as it seems, Tom remembered more about shoes and his hair than anything else that junior year. Tom started to hang his head, talked very little, and shied away from people. He was always looking down at his shoes and wanted the top of his head to be presentable, tilting his face down showing no eye contact with others.

His sister, Marsha had just graduated the year before and had left him a legacy at her graduation. You see; the seniors always had a will read at a special night just before commencement. She had willed to her little brother all the fun and excitement of her junior and senior years spent at Oakbrook. Unfortunately, she had no idea that Tom would be faced with the burdens he bore and the impact it would have on his next two years.

Football practice was well underway and Tom had decided that this is where he was going to find the outlet for the anger, disgrace, and hurt he was harboring inside. The senior class football players were a talented lot. They had speed, quickness, size, and experience. No one on the squad was expecting the juniors to break into the starting line up. At every position there was another senior, just as talented or bigger, waiting to get his shot on the field.

Still, Tom wanted to play and he wanted the opportunity to at least participate. Practices were spent first getting everybody in shape, lots of calisthenics, laps, laps, and more laps. Tom always lacked the speed to be a starter but he did have good reflexes and could react quickly with both feet and hands. At first, when the coaches yelled for underclassmen to grab the dummies or blocking pads, Tom was the quickest and usually the closest to the ground where they were laying. *Then the rest of the drill was spent picking himself up and retrieving the* padded equipment as the running back or lineman barreled over the top of him.

By now, you have the picture; Tom was all of 96 pounds and just five feet tall. By the third practice, Coach Ford called him into his office for a talk. This was coaches' first year at Oakbrook High and they were all very apprehensive. They were not sure what to expect, when you do not know someone other than what has been written about them.

Coach greeted Tom with a big grin on his face. Tom stood in front of him with a wet towel wrapped almost twice around his thin frame. "Tom" he said, "I've been noticing you out there. It gets pretty rough and it's going to get rougher. These boys are big, but from what

I've heard around the league, the other schools' boys are bigger." All the time the coach is talking, he has this big grin on his face and Tom noticed coach's eyes were sparkling, almost wet with tears. Tom is thinking what is wrong with this guy and what did I do?

"So, anyway, what I called you in here for is to ask you how serious are you about this game of football and do you think you can keep up with the pace?"

Tom paused for a moment, to collect his thoughts. What was this guy saying? Was he telling me he couldn't play? Was he telling him he shouldn't play? God, Tom just had to play!

"Coach" Tom stammered, "I . . . I . . . 1 just gotta play! I just got to!"

Coach Ford responded, "Well, Tom, I have to cut this squad down to thirty players by next week. I have to pick from the forty men on the field, those I feel will give all and nothing less. The thirty players I pick will have to endure more physical pain and conditioning than we have experienced this first week. Do you think you are up to that? Do you think you can hold your own and face up to the challenge, no matter what is put before you?"

"Excuse me for interrupting, Coach, but don't cut me. I can do it, I know I can, just let me try and I will show you. Please give me the chance!" Toms' voice had risen to a high pitch. The words were spoken with such truthfulness Tom had surprised not only the coach: but Tom himself. Tom knew he just had to have this time within himself to release the burden he was carrying around. Tom felt tears coming to his eyes.

"O.K., O.K. Lad. We'll give it a few more days and see what happens. You show me your grit and I'll see what I can do. We've got a week and I've got a job to do, too. Good luck and we'll talk again," said Coach.

The next seven days were sheer torture as Coach put all forty boys through ungodly drills, laps, and one-on-one confrontations. All this so he could make that decision which was to be posted on the locker room bulletin board outside Coach Ford's office at 7:00 p.m. Friday.

Tom still pursued the blocking dummies and blocking pads with reckless abandonment. Always, trying to be the first to grab one and consequently always the first to go head over heels in love with the ground on his backside. The final day of practice this week was going to be the day Tom would make the impression that would show the coach and all the others on the team how much he needed to play this game and make the team.

The drill was called the "Meat Grinder". The drill of all drills!! It would go down in history as the most grueling drill ever concocted by a football coach to separate the men from the boys.

Four standup blocking dummies were placed in a square. The front two were placed approximately five feet apart, the back two approximately seven feet apart. The front two placed five feet in front of the back two. It was the unfortunate task of Buck Bronner, the senior Captain of the team and biggest lineman to be selected as the first volunteer. He was to stand in the middle of these four dummies and assume a linebackers position, feet apart, crouched slightly, hands out in front of his body, and head held up. The entire team was directed to line up single file ten paces in front of Buck and one at a time assume a lineman's position. Each member of the team was to be given a three count and then charge Buck to knock him off his feet or out of the square of dummies.

At first, everyone just looked at each other and said this is suicide. No one can stand in there or they will be killed.

So, we started. The first lineman was very cocky and thought he would knock Buck for a loop and dug into the ground with his cleats and threw a few handfuls of grass and dirt behind himself. As he charged Buck he was met with a forearm shiver that sent the lineman on his butt. The next lineman stood there in disbelief, when his butt was met with the swift foot of the coach yelling, "What are you waiting for? Can't you hear me counting to three? One, two, three go!" The next lineman charged, stepping over the first trying to get up. "One, two, three, go!" the coach barked again and again.

This time, Buck was not expecting the onslaught of players all coming to knock him off his feet. The second pushed him back; the third knocked him to one knee; the fourth, fifth, and sixth finished the barrage. The coach jumped in to help the first lineman to his feet and sent him around the far goal post for a lap. Later we found out that the laps were going to be an easy way out of this disaster. The worst form of discipline was an extended tour inside the meat grinder.

As Buck got to his feet, a little shocked, but willing to face more, the coach asked for the next volunteer. You could see everyone grimacing and shuffling to a position where they would not have to have eye contact with the coach. Eyes were being wiped, helmet adjusted, belts being unbuckled, and shoestrings all of a sudden needing to be retied.

Now is my chance, thought Tom. "Me, me, Coach! Let me try?" as Tom scrambled into the open meat grinder. Fastening his helmet that never quite fit right, because his face was so thin that the cheek pads wouldn't touch his skin, Tom dug in with his cleats. Sweat was already running down his arms and hands.

"Well what, do you know, a fly in the meat grinder? Is he a man or a boy? No mercy now you big apes! No mercy! If he is going to play this game he has got to pay the price! One, two, three go! One, two, three go!" Coach Ford exclaimed.

They kept coming one after another. Each bent on nailing Tom to the ground or knocking him out of the meat grinder. All Tom could think of was getting the first one out of the way so he could prepare for the second. And then it was the third before the fourth, and on and on. Tom had used the best advantage he could think of on such short notice and that was to stay low, and this was where he was anyway, at five feet zero inches. Next he would dodge and push with his hands keeping an eye on which leg the opponent was supporting his weight on and moving quickly to his weaker side. Sometimes the lineman would fall flat on his face, sometimes run right on past Tom, and sometimes be knocked off his feet to one side or the other. It wasn't until the sixth lineman came at Tom that he became exhausted and was promptly decked and buried under a pile of arms, legs, and equipment.

Coach Black, assistant coach on the team, walked over after everyone piled off and helped Tom to his feet. He had a big grin on his face, and his eyes were watering more than Tom's.

"Let's go!" Tom yelled, staggering toward the meat grinder.

"Next man in the grinder," coach yelled with his stern voice, as the next combatant entered the meat grinder. Coach Ford glanced over at Tom as he was struggling with his helmet chinstrap and gave Tom his familiar grin. Tom noticed Coach's eyes full of sweat glistening with tears again.

Friday roster was posted right on time. The crowd around the list was tremendous. Most of the seniors who knew they would make the team already were at the front to see whom their fellow teammates would be selected. Tom had butterflies in his stomach and was hesitant to walk across from his locker and fight through the crowd. Tom was so fearful of not seeing his name up there. Whatever would he do if it weren't there? Finally, they all started to disperse and each was congratulating the other or consoling those who got the bad news. Before Tom had a chance to look and find out for himself, Buck Bronner said to him, "Guess we'll be meeting in the meat grinder again, Rooney!"

Sure enough, there it was in capital letters, third from the bottom, TOM ROONEY, defensive safety.

The year was to be full of hard work on the athletic field for Tom, and his academics suffered badly. Tom was holding down a job at a local grocery store, traveling back and forth to school with a car his mom had to share with him. Tom's mother had to work outside the school district, but she made arrangements with the school so Tom could continue to attend Oakbrook High.

The seniors were very good athletes like Tom explained, and the juniors had to accept what they could on the team whenever one of the seniors became injured. In the end, Tom found himself holding the only varsity letter from football after his junior year. Other juniors received varsity letters in basketball, track, or baseball. Tom had also lettered in basketball and baseball.

When the time came to vote for captain of next year's football team the vote was unanimous among seniors and juniors holding varsity letters. Tom Rooney was to lead this band of guys, most twice his size, faster, and most of all they didn't have the problems Tom was still carrying around in his head like a ton of bricks.

Bear Patiently, My Heart, For you
have suffered heavier things, Homer

CHAPTER 2

BAG BOYS, RUMRUNNERS, AND WILD WOMEN

Michigan summer usually start with rain to wash out the spring season of melting snow, dirty lawns, and bring forth lots of crocuses, tulips, and lilacs. It is also said if you don't like the weather today just wait until tomorrow.

Tom's summer was spent working long hours and getting off late at night, either walking home, or sometimes being picked up by the guys after work. There was a break from athletics, and thoughts of the coming school year were put on hold. Events were to happen this summer that almost changed the course of his life.

The summer following Tom's junior year was full of turmoil and confusion. Summer started with Tom's best friend, Bob Warner and he getting jobs at the local grocery store call Handradi's Market. Mr.

Handradi always liked to help out the kids in the town. He not only knew he was helping a kid from going bad but also gaining the respect and patronage of their parents to shop at his store instead of the IGA, his biggest competitor.

Along with Bob, several of their other friends gained employment as well.

They hired in before and were called on to train both of Bob and Tom. There was Terry, Brad, and Tim. We all knew each other from school.

Something strange about Tom's relationship with these co-workers was that although they all came from similar backgrounds, none of them were interested in football the way Tom was. They all dabbled in basketball, baseball, and girl chasing, but none would even try out for football. Bob Warner did try for a short time in his junior year, but dropped out to help his Dad with some heavy equipment company.

Time passed quickly at work, bagging groceries, stocking shelves, sweeping floors and catching hell when they were caught goofing off in the stockroom. They were all young, eager, and full of vigor, like all boys in their teen years. Finally, Tom was assigned to the produce section permanently.

This entailed cleaning the produce and stacking it on display in the store produce section and then keeping the back storeroom clean by throwing out all the empty boxes and produce scraps and damaged products at the end of the night.

After work, the guys all seemed to gather at Brad's house, and everybody always seemed to have a beer or wine. Tom could never see himself, breaking any training rules and never participated in their vices. Tom figured Brad's folks didn't care because they both smoke and drank quite freely anyway. Later, Tom would realize why he was always the first to arrive in his car and why the other guys showed up about a half hour later when they would go to Brad's after work.

The Sunday Tom was supposed to work, was after a pretty wild Saturday night at Brad's. Brad's stepsister and a girl friend had spent the night in their bedroom. Their bedroom door was open and closing all night long with each one of the guys visiting one after the other.

Tom wanted to be accepted by his friends at work but had an attitude that they could live their lives the way they wanted, and beside Tom had enough troubles on his mind and didn't burden his friends about them. He felt pretty much like a wall flower as he would sit with his soda and think about staying in shape for football and wondered when he could get away to run at the track around the football field.

So, on that Sunday, when Tom showed up to work, Mr. Handradi met him at the door. He had a very disturbed look on his face and told Tom to go home. Mr. Handradi wouldn't need him today, and Tom would be hearing from him tomorrow. Tom couldn't believe the luck because he felt lousy from being awake all night, and he wanted to go home and crawl right into bed.

The next day about 11:00 a.m. Tom's Mom picked up the phone and was talking to Mr. Handradi. Tom heard her say something to the affect, "I know Tom would never do anything like that. He isn't that kind of boy. First, don't you think you should get his side of the story? Okay, Mr. Handradi, we'll be hearing from you unless you hear from us first." As she hung up the phone Tom could tell she was about to explode.

"Thomas!" she yelled.

Tom knew he was in trouble by the tone of her voice and her use of his proper first name.

"What have you been up to at work?"

Before Tom had a chance to answer there came another barrage of questions.

11

"What were you boys up to last night? Where did you say you were last night?"

Just as Tom was opening his bedroom door his Mom explained, "You and I have got to talk, right now!"

"Mom, what is this all about?" Tom asked.

"Mr. Handradi says you can pick up your final check this afternoon, young man!" she said to him sternly.

"But, Mom, what is this all about? I haven't done anything!" Tom explained.

"You get dressed right now, and go talk to him. I told him you wouldn't be involved in such stuff. I had better be right or you're in bigger trouble than you can imagine. He says you boys have been stealing booze from the store, and he caught you red handed. He has witnesses!" She said with an angry look on her face.

"Honest, Mom, not me. I don't know anything about booze or stealing anything from Handradi's!" explained Tom.

"I believe you, son, but you have to go up to that store and find out what this is all about, right now!" she said.

So off Tom trucked, scared out of his wits. Tom hadn't been this scared since the railroad detectives caught them throwing rocks at the local freight train. They were on them faster then the boys could get home from the hike they were on. The results were a loss of rank in the Boy Scouts and hard labor in the family garden. But, stealing, this was really serious stuff, and Tom knew he didn't have anything to do with it.

Mr. Handradi was busy with a customer when Tom arrived, so he sat there next to his office like he had been just sent to the principal's office. Perspiration started to form on Tom's forehead and his wet palms were resting on his jeans to try and keep them dry. Finally, Mr.

Handradi was coming toward him with his quick strides and his black heavy eyebrows beginning to curl over his glaring eyes.

"Tom, you have really disappointed me. I never thought of you as this kind of boy. I can't for the life of me understand how you guys thought you could get away with this." Mr. Handradi explained. He was talking so fast Tom didn't have any time to deny or answer any questions. He rushed into his office and came out with a check, handed it to Tom and said, "I don't ever want to see you or any of your friends back in this store again."

Tom looked up at him and the anger in his face. Tom had never been questioned pertaining to his honesty before. This was totally new to him. The reaction shocked him, and Tom just welled up in tears and blurted out, "Mr. Handradi, I never stole from you. I never took anything from you ever. I don't know what your accusing me of, but if it had to do with stealing from you, I did not do it."

Tom turned and ran out of the store, past the cashiers, bagboys, and customers, crying and embarrassed at the thought of being accused a common thief. Once Tom got to the doorsteps of their apartment, his Mom was waiting to hear what went on. Tom explained as much as he knew and asked if he could borrow the car to find out what the other guys had found out. Mom helped dry some tears and said OK, but to call her as soon as he had found out.

The story finally came out, the guys had been stealing wine and beer from the coolers at the store every evening and hiding them in the produce scraps. The crazy thing about it, Tom was helping them by carrying out the boxes filled with what he thought were just scraps and damaged produce each night. Tom would leave early, and the guys would stay late to sweep, mop, and pick up the loot behind the store from the dumpsters. Talk about dumb and naive. Tom was not only that, but also a big sucker, as well. The final result was all the guys got the axe, no criminal charges, and they were never to step foot in Handradi's Market again.

Eventually it took the act of Coach Ford, Tom's principal, several phone calls from Tom's mom, and finally a personal interview and pledge never to give Mr. Handradi any reason to suspect Tom of wrong doing again. Tom held the job for Mr. Handradi until he entered the Army after graduation. Tom would always be grateful for the second chance, and Mr. Handradi's reconfirmed faith in him. Tom had earned his trust and would stop to see Mr. Handradi whenever Tom returned to Oakbrook.

Bob Warner, Tom's best friend, was also fired, but they continued to see each other throughout the summer. It was unfortunate, but Bob and Tom were to have a confrontation at the end of the summer.

Bob had been babysitting children for a neighbor lady. She was a big buxom blonde and was known for her jealous husband. Well, one time Bob stayed overnight at Tom's home after babysitting the night before at the blonde's house. Tom's Mom was home and when the doorbell rang, Bob and Tom were back in Tom's bedroom, so they let mom answer it. There filling up the entire doorway was Bob's neighbor's husband. He was waving this huge gun around and appeared quite drunk.

"Where is that Bob Warner, the rotten little son of a bitch? I'll kill him, I'll kill him!" He slurred through his slobbering mouth.

Tom's mom was pushing him out the door with her hand against his chest as she pleaded, "The boys aren't here. I haven't seen them all day. Get out of here now or I'll call the police!"

Fortunately, one of the neighbors saw the man going up the stairs to the apartment entrance carrying the gun and ran to the police station that was located right behind the apartment building. The police were getting out of their cars as the boys heard the front door slam shut. Bob and Tom were crouched in the hallway, shaking like a couple of scared rabbits.

Bob apologized to Tom's Mom and Tom and decided he should get home as soon as he was sure that crazy man was out of the yard.

He said he would call Tom later to let them know what was going on. Tom told him to tell the neighbor never to come back to the apartment again.

As luck would have it, the man showed up the very next night. Tom's Mom was not home and when Tom opened the door, the man immediately started apologizing all over the place for the way he acted. Tom felt sorry for him. Then he wanted to know where he could find Bob Warner. Tom told him Bob had gone home. Tom told him we had asked Bob never to come back until this mess was straightened out. That's how it was left, and the man excused himself again and again as he went down the stairs.

Tom and his mom were so afraid the man would be back. Although Tom's Mom sensed what it was all about, naive Tom hadn't a clue. As far as Tom was concerned, Bob was wanted for dropping their baby on his head while babysitting.

Tom was to find out shortly thereafter what it was all about in a meeting on a lonely country road. A meeting was to take place between two supposedly good friends who were about to bash each other's head in over a complete misunderstanding.

It was a cool summer night, well lit by a full moon. As Tom turned the '57 Chevy onto Farmers Road from the smooth blacktop of Dixie Highway, Tom heard the gravel spray from the tires. Tom looked in the rear view mirror and noticed another car taking the corner at about the same speed and in the same manner. Then the car lights behind Tom started flashing on and off and the driver was pulling up along side of him. Tom's first thoughts were this is an isolated part of the road and he was by himself. He didn't know what or who was in that car. Suddenly the window came halfway down on the passenger's side and Tom recognized Bob Warner behind the wheel.

He yelled, "Pull over, right now!"

As Tom slowed to a stop, Bob pulled his car in front of the Chevy; half out in the road and pointed toward the ditch. Bob came flying out of his car giving the door a swing as it slammed. He grabbed at Tom's door handle and flung the door wide grabbing Tom by the leather jacket he was wearing. Pulling Tom out of the car he had just enough time to shove it in park, but the car engine was still running.

Bob started screaming, "You son of a bitch! Why did you tell him I was sleeping with his wife? Why did you tell him that?"

By this time Tom was totally taken by surprise and was wearing one of Bob's fist on his upper lip. Then his arm was around Tom's neck and they went tumbling to the ground. Bob was bigger than Tom by about 100 pounds, and all Tom could do was use leverage to roll and try to end up on top. They ended up with both their heads under the back bumper of the '57 Chevy and Tom was still not sure how they got there. Luckily, Tom was the one on top. Bob was stuck. They couldn't get up and Bob couldn't roll over. Tom had pulled his head out from under the car and had hold of Bob's coat lapels. Tom started screaming, "I didn't tell him anything! I didn't tell him a thing!"

Bob started his verbal assault on Tom's heritage and Tom started pulling up on the labels again. This brought great damage to Bob's forehead and definitely brought his submission to reason.

Understand; Bob Warner had always scared Tom with his strength. Tom had seen him lift weights and move cement blocks and really admired his physique. He was no one you wanted to be mad at or worse have him mad at you.

Bob promised to settle down if Tom let him up and then they sat and talked for a while. Tom convinced Bob that what Tom had been telling him was the truth, and Tom didn't even understand until a few punches ago, what the guy wanted Bob for. The two parted that night, on that lonely stretch of Farmers Road, with a handshake and a greater respect for one another.

Bob Warner and Tom saw each other occasionally, but not very often as Tom didn't return to Oakbrook very often. Tom was surprised when he found out Bob named his first child after Tom.

So went Tom's summer of bagboys, rumrunners, and wild women. Gosh, Tom could hardly wait for school to start and he could get back to homework, football, and laps. Tom had never forgotten the heavier burden of hurt, disappointment, and anger he would take into his senior year on the football field.

Remember that you are an actor in a play.
Which the manager directs. Pictetus

CHAPTER 3

COACH

It has been said, that in one's lifetime, some individual will stand out to be very important to you. That individual may change your life, affect your thinking, or just represent someone you could admire or wish to be like.

Before the beginning of the junior year Tom was to meet such an individual that did not only all these things but also many more things for him. This individual would probably not even recall or be aware of how important his influence was on Tom. It is hard to understand but Tom's first recollection was that of fear of this same individual. In just two short years Tom changed this feeling into one of love.

Bill Ford, II was the son of an Italian immigrant and had gained considerable fame on the gridirons of the State of Michigan.

First playing for Guy Houston at Northern High School in Flint, Michigan, his final year was highlighted by a 9-0 season. Bill went on to play for Biggie Munn and Duffy Daugherty at Michigan State University. He culminated his college career on the high note of being named to the 1949 All American College Football Team. Special note being given that he was the smallest lineman ever to be named to an All American Squad.

Bill's first taste of coaching football came on a cool fall night in 1951 in a tiny Upper Peninsula town called Bessemer in Michigan. Bill Ford, Sr., attended the first game and approached his son after the losing battle. He said, "Son, I told you that you were in the wrong racket. Why don't you come back to Flint, and I'll get you a job in the shop and everything will be fine?"

Thank God, Bill refused to quit after the first game. Thank God, he was true to his convictions for love, respect, and hard work for the game of football. Nine years later his record stood at 48-10-5, and Ford received a call from Don Bartow, Oakbrook High School principal.

Mr. Bartow had heard the rumors, read the press releases, and found the increments needed for Oakbrook's floundering football program. He also had a son who would be a senior this year and hoped he would play at Michigan State University. So, in 1960, Mr. and Mrs. Bill Ford II took up residency in the town of Oakbrook, Michigan.

Some of the guys had invited Tom to ride with them up to the football field that summer of 1960. They were just going to throw the ball around and run a little. They were mostly seniors and Tom was more or less just tagging along because he had little talent in comparison to them. If Tom was lucky, he might be able to catch a bad pass or pick up a fumble. After they had run a few 10-yard wind sprints, they gathered to run a few pass plays and play a little on-on-one defense. This is where Tom could get some action. Being too small to be an end or fast enough to be a running back, Tom could keep up with everybody if he played defense. Tom would practice running backwards or shuffling his feet as to not get caught cross-footed, like his older brothers had taught him.

Then, out of nowhere, this stocky old guy came lumbering out on the field. He had gray curly hair, dressed in shorts, his bow-legged and scarred legs protruding down to sweat socks and black athletic shoes. The size of his belly would not allow the MSU sweatshirt to be tucked in and it hung out from his waist. He was the image of an old war house like Joe Padoley, an old ex-pro defensive safety that graduated from Oakbrook and went on to play Pro football. We didn't think it was Joe anyway. Anyway, he grabs one of our footballs and sent Buck Bronner deep for a long pass. Tom didn't think he was ever going to throw it and then all of a sudden the ball is launched in the longest flight Tom had ever seen. It sailed almost seventy yards down the field. Buck hauls it in like it was a baby. If that had been Tom he thought he would have been so dumb founded that the ball came that far and besides it probably would have knocked him down.

As Buck Bronner came back to the group, the old guy says, "You boys all coming out for practice next week?" They all knew they would give it a shot. But, we were all nervous over the new coach that was to arrive this year.

They had all admitted to each other that the rumors they had heard about how tough he was going to be, had them a little timid.

"Yah, sure!" they all chanted.

"How about you, son?" he said as he flipped Tom the football with an underhanded spiral.

Tom stood with his legs crossed, skinny as ever, turning beet red faced, and staggered as the ball arrived.

"Yah, I'll give it a try. But, I'll only be a junior. These guys ahead of me are all seniors and will probably be the starters because they have all the talent. Besides, I weigh all of 96 pounds this year," Tom said.

"What's your name, son?" the old guy asked.

"Tom Rooney, Sir," Tom replied.

"Don't ever let size get in your way, Tom. Sometimes big things come in small packages!" the old guy replied.

"Good. You guys got a nice field here, but it's going to be better. We're going to put new sod down, and surround the field with a fence covered with canvas tarps and make everyone pay to see you play. Well, you boys get back to working out and I'll get back to my job," the old guy departed.

So, off he jogged with those bow-legged limbs and rolling shoulders. They all looked at each other and figured he was some ex-ballplayer hired by the Maintenance Department to rake the field and spruce up the place prior to the school football practice starting this fall.

The following Monday, they were to find the true identity of the maintenance man on the field to be Bill Ford, the new football coach. That Saturday encounter was the very day that was going to become so very important to the rest of Tom's life. The same day that an event was to happen in Tom's life affecting the next two years on the football field and several years later. Not until maturity and a greater understanding of people and life was Tom able to come to grips with this event of that fateful Saturday.

Coach Ford came on like gangbusters. He had brought his own staff of coaches only keeping the baseball coach as a defensive back coach. He had a no nonsense approach and spoke of a determined will to win. He spoke of love for the game; respect for one another, and through hard work the team could attain a winning season. He was here to win because losing had no place in his life. He never liked losing and tie games were like kissing your brother.

His rules were simple. No smoking, no drinking alcohol, no running around late at night, keep your grades up at least passing, and get to bed early. Don't take your helmet off unless you are told to, don't lie down, and work hard all the time. If you had a problem, bring it to him. If you need help, bring it to him. If you have a question, bring it to him. If you want to break the training rules, there was the door. LEAVE NOW!

Practice was to begin every day immediately after school. Uniforms will be issued on a first come first serve basis with seniors, then juniors, and then sophomores or maybe a freshman or two. This didn't concern Tom that much because he knew they didn't have a uniform in the school that would fit him anyway.

They all went to the locker room to be assigned lockers. Seniors got the best lockers in the front of the room near the coach's office. Underclassmen took what was left on the backside of the showers where the other lockers served the visiting basketball teams during basketball season. That's where Tom was issued his locker along with the rest of the underclassmen.

The team was told to line up in the gymnasium, single file, facing the door to the uniform supply room. First they would be weighed and their height measured as they handed in their physical papers that had been completed by their local physician.

As Tom, stepped onto the scale, the defensive back coach moved the slide from 200 Ibs. to 150 Ibs. He then looked at me and said, "Son, are you in the right line?" Then he moved the slide to the 100 Ibs and finally said, "Damn, you are less than 100 Ibs.! It says 96 Ibs.! What are you doing here?" he said.

Tom was embarrassed and said, "I'm here to play football, coach."

"See what we can do for some equipment for this lad," coach yelled to Coach Black in the equipment room.

The pants were the smallest they had (30X30), the shoulder pads were to big but could be adjusted and straps drawn as tight as they could, the thigh pads were to big, and the hip pads would be

22

overlapping in the middle. Then the helmet was the smallest they had a chinstrap that could not be pulled tight enough to have the cheekbones touch the sides of the helmet.

"Good enough for now," said Coach Black, "next!" he yelled

Uniforms were carried home with the belt looped through the equipment and carried with a lot of pride in that you were going out for football. The uniforms had to be laundered, as they were quite stale smelling stored in the storage closet all year. Except for Tom's uniform had to be altered by his Mom. She was a great seamstress and reduced the size of the uniform to fit Tom's 22-inch waist. She worked on all the pads to fit inside the uniform so Tom felt comfortable wearing it.

The very first time Coach Ford called Tom into his office to see if he was able to stay with the game and give it his best effort, Tom knew he liked this man. When coach would get that glassy eyed smile on his face, Tom would feel like he had really reached Tom's heart or true feeling for the game. Tom didn't confide in coach why Tom just had to play the game or just how much coach really meant to him. At times, Tom thought coach knew what was bothering Tom and he knew the right things to say or the time to get Tom distracted onto the business at hand, so Tom couldn't think about the burden he was carrying.

Coach Ford knew each and every one of his boys. He knew about their family lives, their grades in school, their attitudes, and any other problems they may have had in or out of school. Many times the coach and one of his boys or several of them at a time would be having a counseling session in his office. He also never discussed outside the office any thing that went on inside that room, unless there was a need to know. Coach Ford had gained the respect of everyone around the game and also outside the school, such as parents and businessmen.

He was a coach who involved the entire community of Oakbrook in the development of a high school football team. There was advertisement to be promoted for those canvas fences around the football field. Money to be raised for bulletins that needed to be printed and sponsors for programs to be announced during the games. Also, Coach was very friendly toward our local hardware and sporting goods storeowners as he set out to redesign our varsity jackets and to obtain the latest in uniforms and equipment from all of them in the town. He was a promoter who never took no for an answer and never second best for anything.

Tom didn't know how, but he knew the Coach Ford found out all about Tom's heavy burden that was to follow him the next two years. Coach kept it to himself and guided Tom through these difficult years.

Happiness resides not in possessions
And not in gold.
The feeling of happiness swells in the sole Detnocratus

CHAPTER 4

APPEARANCES

Coach Ford knew that appearances mattered in life. When he came to Oakbrook he started to change the appearance everywhere he saw there was room for improvement.

His first goal was to set in motion the rebuilding of the football field. New sod was ordered so it would be ready by the first game in September. He would meet with the Chamber of Commerce and convince the businessmen and women to take out advertisement on canvas panels to be attached to the chain-linked fence that surrounded the football field. In return he promised an increase in their business through local patronage and instructed school officials to direct all their affairs to those businesses that had contributed.

A new Scoreboard was ordered with the team mascot (Wildcat) stretched across the top and electronic lights to be regulated by controls up in the press box were installed. The press box also received a fresh coat of blue and white paint and was divided equally for home and visitor sections. A blue and white railing and ladder for access was installed above the press box to accommodate camera stations as all games were to be recorded.

The field with its new sod would always be freshly striped with sideline marks, hash marks, goal lines, and end zones striped diagonally before each game. The fifty-yard line was divided by a large "O" in script at the center of the field to represent Oakbrook.

Second, Coach Ford looked to the replenishing of the practice uniforms through sale of equipment from other schools around the state. The practice uniforms were always in need of repair and local seamstresses were found to keep them together. The greatest improvement was the new game uniforms. Home field uniforms were white pants and white jerseys with big blue numbers on the front and back. The two blue stripes across each of the shoulders added a nice touch. The away game uniforms had the same white pants and a blue jersey with white number and white stripes across the shoulders.

Coach ordered new helmets for his players that were solid white and had a two blue stripes from back to front. Face guards were optional and were fitted later, most with just a single bar across the face. Chinstraps held the helmet secure and all were lined with foam padding and protected the boys from all those collisions Coach had in store for them.

The team wore white wool socks with blue stripes around the ankles and each team member was to wear black cleats. Linemen wore high tops and running backs wore low cut black shoes with white laces.

Before every game the team members were wrapped in tape around their ankles. Arm pads or finger splints were taped as needed, to protect for sprains, bruises, or cuts. Pre-game preparations allowed for rest, meditation, and game plan study time, after every player had tape applied by their respective coach.

Thursday nights were dress rehearsal and the team all went to the field in complete game uniforms. The first Thursday before the first game as the team entered the newly remodeled football field, they were supposed to run and stop at the fifty-yard line. Instead, the entire team stopped just inside the main gate and just stared in amazement of the whole facility. It was beautiful, plush green freshly mowed grass with bright white chalk lines everywhere. The bleachers glistened with the fresh blue and white paint and sparkled like never before. Surrounding the entire facility were those magnificent white canvas panels, each adorned with encouraging words from local businesses and organizations wishing the team a successful season.

The team just took it all in and then yelled at the top of their lungs as they raced to the center of the field. The team completed the dress rehearsal practice by running a few plays and going over what is expected of each member. After the final gathering all the players thanked Coach Ford and his assistants for the fine job they had done on the football facility. Coach Ford said, "Let's all gather around our captain, Buck Bronner and raise our helmets in the air and yell, GO WILDCATS!!!" This was to be the start of a tradition at the beginning of every game immediately after the coin toss by the captains at the center of the field.

Finally, Coach Ford set his sights on designing a new varsity jacket. The jacket was to be worn only by all those athletes who would letter in a varsity sport, such as football, basketball, track, or baseball. The letter would be given if a player participated in sixteen quarters of varsity football, or sixteen periods of varsity basketball, or placed in the top three of a track event, or participated in sixteen innings of baseball.

To letter in any of the sports was a major accomplishment and elevated the sportsman to a recognizable athlete around the Oakbrook High School campus and community. The athletes were presented their varsity letters for the sport they had earned the required participation at a sport banquet honoring all the athletes at the end of a year. They were also elected into the Letterman's Club on that very night.

Lettering repeatedly in your four year of high school was not heard of, but to letter in your junior and senior years was more of the norm. Many of the high school players wore the metals reflecting this achievement.

First the varsity letter was awarded to the athlete in the sport he was qualified to receive it and a gold pin to be attached to the letter, either in the shape of a football, basketball, track (a foot with wings), or baseball was presented at the same time. A gold bar was given to the athlete who earned a letter in the same sport a second year.

The varsity letter was to be sown to the varsity jacket on the left breast side and was worn with the honor of a general completing many battles over his many years of military service.

Now the varsity jacket was a dark blue wool jacket with two white stripes over the shoulder, like the football jersey. The sleeves of the jacket were made of white leather. The end of the sleeves had blue and white wool cuffs and the waistband and neck collar were of the same color and material. The insulation was heavy for the northern weather in Michigan, but covered with a silk lining inside. The varsity jacket was to promote and display a great pride in the athletic program of Oakbrook High School. The athlete who wore the varsity jacket was always looked up to and praised by lower classmates. The elementary school kids also revered the person wearing one and sought them out to share athletic stories and experiences.

The varsity jacket was seen at fundraisers, school functions, parties, and gatherings outside the school. The person wearing it would always be reminded he was representing the finest of students, a leader, and someone to set the example at Oakbrook High.

Tom Rooney was so proud and humbled as he went into the annual sports banquet. He felt so alone as only a few of his classmates were attending. Don Grayson and Ted Johnson were the only other classmates who lettered in baseball as juniors. Tom was the only junior to receive his varsity letter in football.

The junior year was a turbulent time for Tom. But Tom received a lot of support from Coach Ford and his staff of coaches. The senior members on the football team were also encouraging and thought a lot of Tom during his performance in practices and contributions during the season's games. Coach Ford had picked Tom to receive punts. Tom never took his eye off the ball as it soured through the air from the offensive team punting on fourth down. Tom never fumbled a punt his entire junior year.

Tom's biggest detriment was his lack of speed, and was never able to return a kick for more than twenty yards or less. Still, coach and the team stood by him. Tom remembers the night he entered the game on his sixteenth quarter to earn his varsity letter. When he came off the field after catching a really high end-over-end kick that he could only return for ten yards, because the opponents team was on top of him immediately, all the players applauded. Tom was slapped on the back, helmet, and behind because he had just qualified for his varsity letter.

Heavily and humbly Tom accepted the varsity letter that night of the sports banquet. When his name was announced Coach Ford introduced Tom as the gutless wonder of 107 pounds and afraid of no one. The room full of athletes roared and clapped their approval. It was at that short time Tom felt the deep problem he had been carrying around in his head all year being displaced by the honor given to him that night. He was aware that the varsity jacket would have to wait for him because of all the personal things that were happening in his life that year. No one knew his situation and Tom would hold the problems within himself until he could face them on the football field in his senior year.

He—who submits to fate without complaint, is wise.
Urindes

CHAPTER 5

HEARTBREAK HILL

Returning to school was supposed to be a means of relieving much of the burden building up inside of Tom. He looked forward to the beginning of his senior year and football practice. He had already started conditioning himself at the athletic field along with a few of the other players, who wanted to report in some sort of shape. Tom would run wind sprints, pass the ball around, play some one-on-one pass plays, and run laps. This they thought would prepare them and get a jump on all the other players. Boy, were they in for a surprise!

Coach Ford had a meeting with Tom and his assistant coach Al Black. They went over the general schedule of pre-season training so that they would all be thinking in the same direction. Coach was concerned, decidedly so, and asked if Tom minded if the other players and he could pick a co-captain to help Tom lead the team this year. Tom agreed because he was really beginning to doubt if he was qualified to even make a team let alone captain one. Larry Landon, offensive tackle, was elected and was a tremendous help the rest of the year.

Tom did have the confidence of being the only returning Varsity letterman on the squad this senior year. But, Tom was suffering from a depression and was always troubled by the personal things that had been bothering him since the previous fall training in his junior year. Tom thought Coach Ford could tell something was bothering Tom and he knew the team needed more leadership.

Larry Landon was really a stand up guy. All of the other teammates liked Larry. He was good in school and worked with his dad as a carpenter when not in school. He was built solid and was very knowledgeable about his lineman position as well as all the other positions on the line, defense and offense. Larry and Tom got together and worked on how to teach calisthenics, direct players to assigned drills, and who would coast on this lap while the other led the team up front. Thank God, Tom could never have led this team on every lap. The first day of practice was set up by the devil himself. The temperature was in the 80's, no wind, and dry as a bone. It hadn't rained for the past month. The school was located exactly one mile from the athletic field and every year the team would jog over to the field, run a lap, and wait for all stragglers and the coaches to arrive. Then another lap all together and drills would begin. Not so fast. That was last year and in the past.

This year the community was being invaded by the construction of a shopping center on Mackinaw Street, located one block west of the school. The construction was half completed, and the contractor had conspired with Coach Ford to leave a huge pile of fill dirt and gravel. Between the school and the athletic field was this mound of dirt, topsoil, gravel, and rocks later to be known as Heartbreak Hill.

Coach Ford had an imagination second to none and he devised ways of climbing Heartbreak, crawling Heartbreak, falling down Heartbreak, rolling down Heartbreak, running backwards up Heartbreak, and everything but tearing down Heartbreak Hill. Then

31

the team would not jog the additional mile to the athletic field, but would run full steam until they got there, where they were to make the final lap. Final lap in a pig's eye! One more lap after everyone arrived and then it was on to calisthenics. Tom was one tired varsity letter holder who wanted to kill these teammates for electing him captain.

Larry Landon was in no better shape than Tom was and they both were dragging ass. Coach never let up and pushed them on to do calisthenics. He would walk around the players like a drill sergeant, telling Ray Andrews, how he was going to quit so Coach would not have to cut him from the squad. Fred Baker was a donut factory that was about to explode. One after the other Coach made the first day out a living hell. Coach knew exactly what he had to do. He had to prepare a team within four weeks, physically fit, mentally alert, and positively team oriented.

On the other hand, the first day to the players was just concentrated on how to make it through the practice and stay alive. Most of the guys had already given up their cookies on the first lap after everyone had arrived. Others would interrupt calisthenics and start calling, "Ralph!" through their headgear as they knelt down or rolled over. Oh yes, the coach instructed everyone the helmets were not come off for the first week! After a series of wind sprints by the whole team, they were divided up into three groups: linemen, backs, and underclassmen. Finally, they would try some one-on-one drills, and Tom could maybe release some of the frustration and anger inside him. Wrong again! Wind sprints by the clock held by Coach Ford to see who was the fastest. Tom whispered to Larry Landon, "Hell, this is to see who has survived!" It was no surprise to find sophomore Abe Boady to be the fastest player on the team.

Abe Boady, an old farm boy, later to become All-conference for the next three years was a coach's dream. Abe was recruited by Coach Ford and moved up to the varsity team and all he had to be taught was how to carry a football. He was as strong as an ox and could carry the weight of one also. Naturally, he was playing left halfback on offense. Tom's position whenever they need him on offense that is.

The smell of upchuck was starting to get to everybody when a loud voice from heaven was heard. It was that of Coach Ford, as he bellowed, "I'll meet you all back over at Heartbreak Hill in about fifteen minutes!"

Again, they met, attacked, and conquered Heartbreak in every way possible. The jog back to the school and the showers was like crossing the great desert and many just sank on the grass outside, too tired to take off their cleats, some just laid motionless or waited for their turn to spray the garden hose on their filthy dirty faces and drink some water. Tom went directly to the locker room and knew that the only way to become alive again was getting out of this uniform and into the hot shower followed by a cold spray. Finally, Tom didn't mind being first.

They all finally made it through practices the first week and things got down to a pretty smooth routine. Three weeks away from their first opponent and they were all feeling pretty sure of themselves and what they had accomplished. Heartbreak was always there everyday, but now they knew what to expect and how to pace themselves.

Tempers would flare once in awhile because the competition to make the team was tremendous. The talent was deep and many underclassmen had a good chance of starting this year. Tom was resolved to stay on defense and concentrate on studying the opponent's offensive plays. Here was his home and Tom would dispense his anger and revenge for the problems he carried.

The Meat Grinder came and went. The one-on-one drills came and went. The laps became easier and easier and fast was approaching the final week before the first game.

Larry Landon was appointed offense captain, who worked fine since he was on offense, and Tom was appointed defense captain. Tom was also chosen to receive punt and kickoff returns. An unlikely choice because Tom wore those darn glasses that seem to always get in the way or were broken and taped together at the nose. Coach Ford told Tom he wanted him on both of these positions because he knew Tom would only go in one direction—straight up the field.

Tom said to coach, "As slow as I am, it was the quickest way to the End Zone!"

Anyway, with all these obstacles, Tom still never took his eyes off the ball and never fumbled a reception.

The first opponent was Parkville High. It would be a home game for Oakbrook, and Tom was so looking forward to their meeting. During Tom's sophomore year on junior varsity, Ted Simms, the present quarterback for Oakbrook, had hurt himself and was out for the season. Good old naive Tom volunteered to become the one and only quarterback. Well, Parkville found out that Oakbrook had only Tom and he was greeted at the end of each and every play by one or two of those bastards whether he had the ball or not.

When Tom complained to the referee he was told, "Welcome to the quarterback position." Tom came out of that game so black and blue; he couldn't make practice until Wednesday of the following week. Tom had to soak in the whirlpool to heal his injuries and bruises.

Thanks to Abe Boady, with the help of a lot of other fine blockers, and the confidence they had as a team, Parkville fell to Oakbrook, 30-13. The first four weeks of hard work paid off and the team basked in its glory. Coach Ford let up and they all felt there were going to be some great times ahead.

Remember, no human condition is ever permanent,
Then you will not be overjoyed in good fortune,
Nor sorrowed in misfortune. Isocates

CHAPTER 6

MEMORIES

The record of that 1962 Oakbrook High School football team was nothing to brag about. Yet, Coach Ford was to later say that the record of a team does not always represent the measure of success. It was a season of three wins and six close losses. Most of those losses could have been turned around on a single break or play. As players, they all learned more through just playing on the team and being guided by one of the greatest coaches ever to coach at the high school level.

The satisfaction of the first victory against Parkville was short lived. Because of over confidence and under estimating their opponent the following week Oakbrook went down to a 0-17 defeat at the hands of Pearson High. Pearson was a seasoned team having so many returning lettermen, and Oakbrook was still making mistakes due to the lack of field experience. Pearson appeared twice on the schedule as the Oakbrook players had hopes of a win at the second confrontation.

Coach Ford decided his team needed to be tested by a higher powerhouse after their defeat by Pearson. Coach's old high school, where he excelled as a lineman was located just south of Oakbrook in the largest city around. The school was rated as a Class AA football program. Oakbrook High was rated as a Class B football program. Coach Ford had arranged for his Oakbrook team to scrimmage this team.

As we boarded the bus to travel that Tuesday practice night, all the guys from Oakbrook were pretty nervous. The team members were discussing the articles they had read in the local newspapers. The opponent had an average line weighing in around 250 lbs. per man, and their running backs were all bigger than Oakbrook's linemen, averaging 180 to 200 lbs.

Getting off the bus Oakbrook players were greeted by a host of cheers and laughter. It was apparent from the beginning; Oakbrook was out weighed, out run, and out played, as they got back on the bus to go home.

Coach Ford would only say, "You guys did yourself proud, and they weren't all that bad."

Wednesday practice the Oakbrook boys ran a bit faster, hit a bit harder, and worked longer than before. The experience of playing a Class AA team worked just like Coach Ford had hoped it would.

The next game was to be against a school called Barkley. They were sporting the return of an All-conference wide receiver; he was later to go on to college and become an All-American and later play Pro ball for the Minnesota Vikings. Tom's older brother had run track against this kid and he warned Tom not to let the guy ever get behind him or so long.

Tom spent extra long hours in front of game films Coach Ford always had available on opponents they were to play. The offense Barkley was running seemed centered on this tall lengthy guy who Tom remembered looked more like a stork. One thing for sure, if the ball came anywhere near him, he would score.

This guy would usually leave the defensive back, falling on the ground at the line-of-scrimmage as he would fake the poor guys out of their jock straps with his moves. Even with his lengthy body he seemed to be able to shift one way and yet go the other. The arms would go east and the legs went west. But, one thing Tom had been taught in his junior year on varsity, the waist never moved unless the legs followed. The waist would always go in the direction the player would go. With this in mind and one other trick Tom had up his sleeve, Tom had a talk with Coach Ford.

During practice the Oakbrook team was going to take on the Barkley receivers, played by underclassmen. The coach chose Rob Peterson to play the stork. Tom was assigned to cover him. Rob was built just like the stork.

So as the practice proceeded Tom used all the skills and ideas he had to contain this monster.

The All-conference receiver was good, and it wasn't just all hype. He would be faster than Tom if he were running backwards. He was taller than Tom. Tom's helmet didn't even come to the top of his shoulder pads.

Now, part of Tom's scheme was home field advantage. Being captain, Tom would always go out for the coin toss at the beginning of each game. It was quite a scene as Tom met this monster that was all of 6'11" at center field—kind of like the David and Goliath from the bible. Now, it wasn't just a coincidence that one of the referees was an alumnus of Oakbrook High and had played on the famous un-scored-upon team with Tom's oldest brother.

When Tom approached them, the referee gave Tom a friendly wink. Oakbrook won the toss, everyone left but the referee and Tom. He leaned down patting Tom on the behind and then Tom whispered his plan of attack to referee. He said in a reassuring voice, "I think you guys will do O.K."

Tom was not saying this game had a fix on it, but Oakbrook played very hard and deserved to win. Most of all, everything Tom did to the stork worked like perfection. Once, late in the second half, they caught Tom for holding the monster. It was a small price to pay for a scoreless halftime for the visitors.

Tom's strategy was to never take his eyes off this guy's belt buckle. Give him enough distance as to not let him get behind Tom. Except, when Tom would deck him before he could get off the line of scrimmage by falling down in front of him or hitting him as if Tom were blocking him. This kept him totally confused and gun shy the entire game. Tom watched him leaving at half time, limping badly and shaking his head; Tom knew he was winning the battle.

The rules of the game have changed considerable since the sixties. The helmet is no longer permitted to make a tackle. With Tom, if he had to use just his shoulder pad, there would not have been enough space for a thigh or another part of the human body to fit his small shoulder pads. The helmet was Tom's main source of strength. It was able to bruise more shins, penetrate more stomachs, or crack more opponent's helmets and sometimes his own. Also, the art of knocking the receiver down was legal then but is not allowed today.

Barkley's star player never caught a pass, tried several end around sweeps, and most importantly never scored. Some of the burdens and pressure Tom felt were relieved during this game, and he felt good about accomplishing a goal he had for himself. The team was ecstatic being 2-1 so far and they were all looking forward to their next challenge.

So who do you think they should come up against? The next opponent was the powerhouse team who eventually won the conference that year. 38-0 was the final humiliation. One cracked helmet and one pair of glasses snapped in half again. Coach helped Tom tape together the glasses during a sideline time out so Tom would not miss a play. Just as Tom was running back to the huddle, the guys told him to get off the field. They had already sent in a sub. When Tom got back to the sidelines, he noticed blood dripping off his face. The glasses had cut a gash in the bridge of his nose and with just a band aide and Tom was ready to go. Oakbrook played hard, but the team was just extremely outclassed.

The following week was to be against neighboring Southville High School. Known for the many talented black players, they boasted a 300-pound fullback. Everybody on Oakbrook's team was thinking about trying to tackle this beefcake. Coach assigned our biggest lineman, Buck Bronner, to play fullback during practice all week. Buck got a kick out of it and the players got a lot of bruised shoulders, necks, and arms. Later the team was to find out what hitting a real 300-pound running fullback felt like.

Oakbrook was able to get an early jump on them with their hard running halfback, Abe Boedy. The end of first quarter found Oakbrook leading by 13-0. Then all hell broke loose. The shoot was opened and they let out the bull. He hit like a Mack truck. His ankles were as big as Tom's thighs. He cracked Tom's helmet, and Tom was knocked out for a short time. The 300-pound running back had been driven back into the end zone on the play, but the ball was set on the one-yard line. They were forced to kick on fourth down, but Tom was not to receive the kick because he was counting stars on the sideline. Tom was back in the game on the next defensive series, but had to wear someone else's helmet. The helmet didn't fit, but neither did that 300-pound body fit up against Tom's body. The rest of the game was all Southville's ending on a 33-13 note. Now Oakbrook was 2-3 overall.

The next game was the rematch against Pearson. Oakbrook was much better but not good enough. Oakbrook went down 19-2. The score did not represent how hard Oakbrook played against this team. Tom's only excuse was he was probably looking past Pearson to the game against our archrival Clover. More importantly, Tom's cousin, Jerry Prey, was a track star and wide receiver for them. He also played punt return specialist and had built himself a reputation with his speed. Tom was the punt return specialist for Oakbrook, but he had no speed or reputation.

Jerry Prey was thin and small also, but still outweighed Tom by 20-pounds. What the hell? Everyone outweighed Tom anyway. Tom had always remembered Jerry as a shy quiet type of guy. Very nice and polite but loved to run. Cross Country, track, and that kind of stuff was where he kept his interests. Tom never knew him to like football though.

Jerry and Tom both met before the coin toss on the thirty-yard line to wish each other a good game and good luck. Tom said, "Look out, I'm going to get you." Jerry replied, "Only if you can catch me!" They shook hands as the crowds in the stands where cheering and clapping for them. My teammates joked with me about kissing him instead of shaking his hand. Tom told them to watch when he would kiss Jerry the first time he ever carried the ball. Somehow, that came natural to Tom when he played an opponent. Once, on the field, Tom would respect the opponent, but like him—never!!

Oakbrook went on to win the game against Clover by the score of 20-7. Jerry Prey got the only touchdown. Tom never got close enough to kiss him, but he did meet him in the end zone to shake his hand and tell him what a good run it was.

The next week found Oakbrook overmatched, but yet against a very powerful eleven from Grand Bay. They posted a 19-6 victory against Oakbrook. Even in defeat Oakbrook felt good because they played to the best of their abilities. The Grand Bay game was their second-to-last game of the season. To the seniors, time was running out, and they were looking at a losing season. More importantly, they were looking at an end of four years of dedication, training, and the opportunity to play this game.

This game, win or loose, meant so much to Tom personally. It was a release of things stored up inside of him. A way to express himself in the best way he knew how. It was so much easier to run and hit as hard as he could. Explode into the other player so hard and know he would get up and walk away. After all, they had all that equipment to keep them protected. The game had to mean so much to Tom, and not because losses were so gut—wringing the tears would always come and he couldn't hold them back. Tom felt that he had let Coach Ford down, the team down, and himself down, as he felt the loss was his fault. The burden and problems still plagued Tom enough to bring him back to another practice, another opponent, and another opportunity to strike back.

The last game was going to be very special to Tom, and he planned on giving it every ounce of his being. Coach had let them know the last game is the one you will always remember. He was right, but Tom still remembered the other as well, just not as clearly as the last one. The game was against Daniel High. Their captain was 10 pounds heavier than Tom. They were fired up to end their season on a winning note, and Oakbrook was just as determined.

CHAPTER 7

HOMECOMING

High school football always has a week of Homecoming, and Oakbrook High was no different. The week was filled with all kinds of activity. The girls put on a football game complete with gear and the boys wore cheerleading outfits dressed up like girls. There was the process involving elections to choose a Homecoming Queen, and that particular year Oakbrook decided to elect a Homecoming King as well. The different classes were to elect female students to represent their class as part of the Homecoming Queen's court. The classes were busy decorating floats for a parade in town. Then during the halftime there would be another parade of the floats and a prize given to the best one. At this time the results of the elections were announced and the Homecoming Queen and King were crowned.

The Queen of Homecoming that year was the beautiful red head, Janet White, and the King was offensive receiver Ben Markel. The

Homecoming dance that would follow the game was also a big deal. A lot of planning went into preparation for the dance, and all seniors were to attend.

Tom was hurting and really suffering with the burden he was still carrying around and tried to concentrate on the big game against Barkley. Fortunately, the game was a victory for Oakbrook. Earlier in the weeks leading up to Homecoming, Tom was really not interested at first in going to the dance. Yet, he was still trying to hide his humiliation and disgrace that had been plaguing him since his junior year. Then there was the dinner after the dance where you were supposed to take your date.

Tom built up the nerve just two weeks before the Homecoming to ask Christine Baker. Christine was the lead cheerleader on the team that year. Christine hesitated for a moment and then said yes, she would go with Tom.

Tom's older brother, Gary gave him his Oldsmobile to drive, as Tom's Mother needed the '57 Chevy that weekend. So plans were made to double date with another couple, split the gas, and travel to Canada to have dinner.

Tom had a past relationship with Christine just prior to an event in Tom's life that would give him much pain and anger. It was back in the fall before his junior year and the Gloski twins, Don and Glenda, gave a party held at their home. Glenda Gloski kept after Tom to be sure and attends because Christine was expecting him and she wanted to meet him there.

It was a great party as Tom recalled and was attended by just about everyone in the class. The Gloski home was very crowded, and Tom remembered kids running in and out all night long. The best part was the Gloski party was un-chaperoned and there was a lot of beer, music, dancing, and petting going on, all the favorite pastimes of the start of 60's.

The party provided a long awaited opportunity for Toms' first adolescent sweetheart, Christine Baker, to set her objectives and snare her target: Tom!

This was nothing Tom was not already aware of, nor did he have any contrary feelings toward Christine accomplishing her goal. Christine was always attractive, popular, and as Tom was later to find out that evening, great at making out.

The party was well on its way when Tom arrived via his mother dropping him off. Of course, every parent was assured, as Tom's Mom was, the party would be well chaperoned, and smoking and drinking were definitely out. The kids were all so very convincing back then.

As Tom entered the living room, Glenda Gloski immediately came to greet him and said Christine wanted to see him in the kitchen. Tom's heart did a couple of flips, and he shyly shoved his hands into his pockets and turned a bright red. There followed a lot of Oh's and Ah's and then the giggles and tee-hees. Everyone knew of the notes and whispers that had circulated back at school with the highly classified messages. Does she like him? Does he like her? Does she want to go to the party with him? What do you mean, you don't know how to ask her?

Slowly, Tom made his way to the kitchen to find Christine sipping on a straw stuck in a bottle of Coke. Her eyes looked up to meet Tom's eager blushing face, and she had him sweating profusely on his neck and palms.

As she offered to share the Coke, she spoke so assuredly and self confidently, "Tom, want some soda?"

The best intellectual utterance Tom could muster was, "Yup."

They made some social small talk, that Tom could remember, and about the only thing Tom came up with was, "Boy, it sure is hot in here! How about going for a walk outside?"

Now Tom really meant that. It was hot and the sweat was still trickling down his arms; the Old Spice wasn't doing so well; and his palms were getting the inside of his back pockets pretty wet.

This was just the invitation Christine had been waiting for. Just a slide and a step and she had him right where she wanted him. Can't say Tom wasn't feeling better away from all the staring eyes, but the breeze outside felt a lot better. Christine took charge right away and started to speak of her admiration for Tom, and she hoped that Tom felt the same way toward her. This was truly Tom's first time he had anyone of Christine's beauty and personality ever talk to him like she did. She really opened up to him and spoke as truthfully as possible. Tom admired her for her truthfulness, even though he couldn't for the life of him understand what she saw in this bashful, quiet, scrawny kid.

As inexperienced as Tom was, he guessed, he handled the situation pretty good because before the night was over they had necked pretty heavily, behind the house, on the side of the house, against the school wall next door, and ended up on the couch in the living room in front of everyone to end the party.

Christine was probably the sweetest girl Tom had ever known at this stage in his young innocent life. Tom did not want to intentionally hurt her in any way, but hurt her he did. They left the party separately that evening, Tom promised to call her the very next day. Saturday, he awoke with all intentions of calling Christine bright and early that morning. Then Tom couldn't make up his mind what to say to her. Then he was afraid she might want him to make a date with her to go to a movie or something. Then he started worrying about her parents and his parents. Tom knew her parents were happily married and his parents fought continuously. Finally, he convinced himself, it would never work and he was way over his head in thinking this girl could ever like someone like him, someone who couldn't even bring himself to call her on the phone. Sunday came and went. Tom had the entire day to make the call, but didn't.

Monday came and Tom knew he would see Christine in school. The halls seem to be a buzz about the great party at Gloski's. Everyone was bragging about their exploits of drinking more, or being the loudest, most obnoxious, or whatever. Finally, someone made a crack to Tom about how close Christine and Tom had gotten. Tom turned on his heels and walked away, knowing he felt terrible about not keeping his promise to her.

Christine was standing with a bunch of her girlfriends talking in low whispers. There wasn't the usual giggles and laughs in their conversations. When she looked up to see Tom, she burst into tears and ran into the girls' bathroom with two or three of her friends following. Someone said, "Tom, why didn't you call her?"

Tom couldn't answer, and he felt like the lowest form of life as he turned to avoid them all.

Tom spent the rest of the year trying to avoid Christine. They never talked about it again, and Tom lost a lot of respect among the rest of the kids in his class. In losing so much, Tom became quite lonely, talked to fewer friends, and pretty much became a loner. He really cared for Christine and would never get over her the rest of his school days. Many times Tom had wanted to explain to her the reasons he never called, and they were never very close after that. Tom didn't really blame her for feeling the way she did. She must have felt betrayed and used. Tom felt ashamed and unworthy. They both stayed away from each other to avoid a confrontation.

Almost two years had passed and the Homecoming was coming up. The Homecoming was one of the highlights of the senior year, and Tom was trying his best to experience everything good about this final year in school Tom also was trying to fight against the burden that was overwhelming him on the football field. Maybe going to the Homecoming dance would help to keep his mind off that burden.

Now, Christine Baker had not let her first romance with Tom Rooney keep her from pursuing the many other candidates in the class. The senior year found her courting Larry Landon, co-captain on the varsity football team and Terry Schram, captain of the debate team.

Terry Schram was one of the most likeable guys in school. Liked by not only all the guys, Terry was liked by most of all the girls. Terry had a way of making everybody feel at ease. He knew just the right things to say and do. Girls really liked that about Terry. He could handle himself in any situation. Sometimes, it would be the right gentlemanly gesture or in most cases the comical response was just at the right time to crack everyone up hysterically.

Larry Landon was one of the good guys. One of the boys every mother would be proud of having their daughter date. He was very fair, hard working, average grades, clean cut, and just a nice guy. Larry was a lineman on the football team and grew to be a pretty average leader as well. Without Larry, Tom would have had a rough time of leading the Varsity football team alone.

It seems like a scene from the soap operas, Christine was going with Larry, but they had just broken up and she was seeing Terry. Now, Terry had become interested in a girl called Judy Jones. Anyway, in comes Tom to ask Christine to be his date for the Homecoming dance.

Honestly, Tom felt Christine Baker was looking for a way to make Larry Landon jealous. At any rate, she said she would go and they set out to match the outfits, arrange transportation, and make plans for the grand evening.

She picked out a lacy full gown, and Tom went with a bunch of guys to pick out a tux. The cumber-bun had to match the color of the gown Christine wore. Tom also arranged for a corsage. Tom's oldest brother, Gary let him borrow his car for the special evening. Tom planned to drive to Canada and meet a bunch of our classmates at a swanky restaurant called Fisherman's Wharf.

All this took place in the three weeks prior to the actual Homecoming. By the time the Homecoming night arrived, it was decided Christine and Tom would double date with Terry Schram and Judy Jones. The rest of the plans were intact and Tom would do the driving.

But wait, now for the ringer. As things would happen, Christine Baker had now been seeing Terry Schram on a regular basis. Judy Jones was looking elsewhere, and Tom was still wrapped up in his football. Oh well, they were all bound and determined not to let this stand in their way of having a good time. They were all aware of how each other felt and realized that everyone had made all those plans. So, off they went to celebrate their victory over Barkley High and their senior Homecoming.

Christine looked lovely when Tom picked her up. From her house, they went over to pick up Terry Schram. Tom was a little taken back when those two kissed after they got in the car. That had to be a first. Then they went over to pick up Judy Jones and that old smooth Terry Schram snuck in a kiss from Judy while Christine wasn't looking. Boy, he was good!

All during the dance, Christine and Tom would dance maybe one or two dances and then she was gone. Tom would act as if it didn't bother him, and he would get into deep conversations about the game against Barkley and the "stork." Once, Tom noticed Christine and Terry over in a corner, holding hands and then on the dance floor. Everyone knew the crazy triangle they all found themselves in and thought they were all just crazy.

Tom personally felt he was getting everything he deserved for the way he treated Christine back in their sophomore year.

One of the funniest things Tom will always remember about that evening was their trip to Canada for dinner. They were required to pass over the bridge that led to Canada and through customs. On the way over everything went well, but on the way back the Americans were quite liberal the Canadian Mounted Police asked all kinds of questions. Unfortunately, for Christine Baker, when she snapped back a smart answer at the Mounted Police Officer, he jerked to attention and asked them to step out of the car. They all took it as a joke at first, and then he became quite angry. Now, they knew he was serious, and they started to think of the trouble they could get into. Not that they were hiding anything, but the Canadians could detain them for quite awhile.

The Mounted Police Officer asked Tom to open the trunk. Tom nervously fumbled with the keys, and the officer asked him to step back. Seeing the suitcase in the trunk, the officer asked whom it belonged to. Christine was going to spend the night with Judy and so she brought along the suitcase. "Open it up!" the officer demanded.

They all lined up behind the trunk and <u>Sergeant Preston</u> proceeded to display the prettiest silk nightgown and underclothing Christine Baker owned. She was very embarrassed and apologized for being abusive toward the officer.

The next day, Tom called Christine Baker at Judy's house only to find that she wasn't there. At least Tom called and felt he had made an effort.

Years later, Christine Baker married Larry Landon and lived happily ever after. Terry Schram married another girl and then another.

Every man will fall who,
Though born a man,
Proudly presumes to be a superman.
Sophocles

CHAPTER 8

THE FINAL PEP RALLY

The noise of clattering seats, shuffling of feet, whistles, yelling, all familiar sounds of some 500-plus students and faculty making their way to our final football season assembly was elevated by the school's circular construction with a gymnasium in the center surrounded by a overhead balcony. The gathering had been repeated just seven days earlier as they always had done for a pep rally before the Friday night game. This being the final pep rally was to be a little more special, so school was called off at 1:00 p.m., and everyone was to attend.

Oakbrook High School was uniquely designed in that it was two story round structure with the exception of the library and administration offices, jutting off from a hallway to the north as a separate wing. Tom always thought the building as representing the biological symbol for the male species.

The gymnasium served as the auditorium with a balcony surrounding the room about eight feet above the walls. The opposing teams entering the basketball court always complained of the echoes they would hear when they reached half court. Many times, the referee would blow a whistle for a double dribble or loss of possession on the opponent. That was called home court advantage.

When everyone found whom they wanted to sit next to or away from, the usual process of quieting the student body began. Finally, one of the cheerleaders got a senior group to start the school fight song. The song always ended with a rousing round of applause. That is when the high school principal Mr. Bartow stepped to the microphone and began to speak.

"Seniors . . . (followed by loud round of cheers, applause, and stomping of their feet), Juniors . . . (followed by a louder round of the same), Sophomores . . . (followed by an enthusiastic but much more quiet group), and Freshman . . . (a crazed mixer of boo's applause, yells, and hisses) welcome to the Final Football Season Rally of 1961!!" he bellowed.

The cheerleaders responded with leading the entire group in another chorus of the old fight song.

Again, the principal waited for the applause to die down and went on to say, "Without further ado, I give you the best football coach in the Big Eight Conference, Coach Ford!"

That was our principal. Always short, quick, and to the point; he did have our respect because he also wheeled a pretty mean paddle back then when it was acceptable.

Coach Ford. What a man! What a coach! He was an All-American pulling-guard from Michigan State University in 1949. Worshipped by all his players, and cursed by all of his players at some time in his tutelage. Loved by all and feared by many. Rough speaking with his gravely voice but had sparkling eyes that became tearful when he was touched by something he felt deeply about. Yes, Coach Ford was a man Tom grew to love, respect, idolize, and would have given his last breath of strength to satisfy Coach's will to win. But, win or lose on the field, he was truly a winner among men.

The applause was thunderous and longer than expected by all. The season had not been very boastful or glorious, but the admiration of this man was overwhelming for the quietest of student or faculty member.

He stood before them, bow-legged from old, bruised, football injuries with eyes sparkling of gratitude, and raised arms asking for a moment to speak. They all knew it would be more than a moment. This man could speak like no other coach they had ever had at Oakbrook. He could inspire, calm, excite, and most of all bring smiles to tears-soaked faces, or promises of success to fallen hearts.

Coach raised his arms gesturing to all before him, looking around the auditorium, "Students of Oakbrook High School. I welcome you all and thank you all for your spirit, support, enthusiasm, and most of all for your loyalty and strength."

Oh he was a crowd pleaser and orator par excellent.

"Like Mr. Bartow has stated, 'this is our last football season rally.' But, it is much more than that, so much more than just a last rally. This is more importantly a meeting for the last time of a group of individuals who have banned together to become a team capable on any given night, facing an opponent, and when playing at their very best attainable level, defeat that opponent. Through endless hours on and off the field they each have struggled, academically, physically, and mentally, to prepare for a challenge against an opponent equal to the task. Each time one or the other will come out a winner according to the scoreboard. Let me tell you now; the scoreboard does not always tell the final story. The winners are on both sides of the ball in the larger sense of the game. This is how I will look back at this year and these men I am so proud of and I am about to introduce to you. They are all winners!"

Coach introduced Assistant Coach Al Black and the team manager, Harvey Wise, who was also a senior.

Followed by a round of cheers and applause, Coach Ford introduced each and every player starting from the underclassmen. Each one was singled out for some achievement, no matter how insignificant, showing the coach's interest in each of his young men. Finally, he came to the seniors. He paused, "It is with much pleasure I now introduce the seniors of your 1962 Oakbrook High School Football team."

Another round of cheers and applause, pronounced from the section holding the majority of senior classmates.

Coach said, "Let me first say to these young men, they are about to begin an evening that will live with them throughout their lives. They shall never play this game of football on an organized level again. The final game is in most cases the one that stands out from all the rest. That final score, or final play, each and every part of the final game will be remembered and thought over and over again. Because it was the last time they were part of this team."

The silence seemed to last forever as Coach Ford's words hit Tom like a ton of bricks. All week Tom had been going through the motions of the routine practice maneuvers and toyed with the ideas of what was he going to do next week without football or how nice it was going to be to go home after school and just relax. The thought just sank in that Tom was going to be devastated and wanted to give this last game everything he had so he could go out a winner and have a winning game to remember for the rest of his life.

"Starting tackle, mean and rough across from the best of opponents and holding his own, Dan Gloski!" Coach asked for the applause to be held to a brief acknowledgment, as they will never be able to get through on time. Still each senior received his honored response from the student body.

"Jake Arons has been one of the hardest working men on our team this year and deserves his starting position tonight on this last season. Ray Andrews will be giving Jake his share of bench time as these two compliment our guard positions. Also in reserve we have Joe Wilson and John Stokes who have helped tremendously this week, acting as our opponents on defense. One of the best pulling guards I have had the pleasure of teaching the game, from a position I have grown very fond of over the years, I give you Dan Cracker. The tackle position next to our guards will be ably handled by senior Johny Street and Co-captain Larry Landon who have helped to lead this team through many successful moments as well as helped to lift them through their defeats. I want to introduce the center of this senior line, which is solid with the talents of Dennis Blake and Bob Smith. Last but not least, another end with talents displayed throughout this year, I give you Ted Johnson. Our halfbacks are second—string Kyle Freeman and All-conference Doug Betters. Quarterbacks are known for their leadership, daring, and knowledge of the game. We all know there is only one man left with these talents, and I introduce you to Tommy Schoemaker."

Coach now pauses and asks for a round of applause. The student body responds on cue. Coach joins in to assure he gets his lengthy pause he orchestrated.

Coach says, "It is now time I introduce to you a young man you all had the pleasure of knowing as a fellow classmate, friend, teammate, and maybe hero. You have read about his prowess on the field in our local papers recently (making reference to a full page article in the week's largest newspaper about the smallest captain in the Big Eight Conference). You have seen some of the unexplainable confrontations on the field against opponents twice his size. Some of these, fellow players have felt his impact, dodged his path of pursuit, or picked themselves up after failing to get passed him."

There was a rustling among the student body in the bleachers, and whispers could be heard as the coach was starting to speak again.

He said, "I have coached many young men through out my years. I have had All-state players, all-conference players, a lot of 200-pound players, and one 300-pound player, but to this date none with the heart and love for the game as this young man. He has exemplified the tenacity of a true player of the game even though he lacked the speed and size to play the game. He has shown to us the game of football can be played by a small man, if the desire and guts are there. What I will never be able to understand is the young man has no gut. He has a 22-inch waist. We have to tape his pants on him to hold them up. Soaking wet he will tip the scale at 117 pounds at the beginning of a game and weigh in at 107 pounds by the end of the game. I have never until this past two years had the pleasure of knowing and coaching such a young man. I will always remember him as the Gutless Wonder. Ladies and gentlemen, I introduce to you the Captain of your 1962 Oakbrook Wildcat Football team, Tom Rooney, the Gutless Wonder.

Look death in the face with joyful hope,
And consider this a lasting truth:
The righteous man has nothing to fear
Neither in life, nor in death,
And the gods will not forsake him.
Socrates

CHAPTER 9

THE LAST RUN

The snowfall was just starting to lighten, and the flakes were big and puffy. The blanket of snow had grown to about two feet deep. Plows had begun to clear the streets under the light of a full moon. This was a beautiful time in a very long winter season. These evenings were few among so many of the blizzard cold, dark, or sloppy nights of our Michigan winters. So, naturally when one of these perfect nights came along they would want to take advantage of the perfect conditions.

The phone rang just once, and Tom knew it would be one of the guys. It was Terry Schram. The guys had all gathered at his house and wanted to know if Tom could join them for a night of tobogganing. They all knew that Tom had one of the best eight-foot sleds around and also the transportation. Tom was still sharing a pretty red and white '57 Chevy with his mom, Becky.

The biggest, and only, problem for Tom was he would have to go by his father's house to pick up the toboggan. So, Tom called him first and asked if he would mind setting it outside, and he would be there to pick it up. The answer was stern but positive and the situation was half solved. When he pulled into his father's driveway, the toboggan was waiting, and his dad was standing there with a rope to help secure the sled to Tom's car. The last thing his father said was, "Won't you come back home, when you bring the sled back?"

It was funny, that now, after football season, Tom had gone back to running around with the old crowd who used to work at Handradi's Market. They would all talk about the old days of bootlegging and how dumb Tom was about the whole situation.

At least now, Tom was having an occasional beer with the guys, even though he never acquired a taste for the brew. He could join in their antics of bragging on how much he could consume and lie right along with the best of them. They were all good guys who just made their mistakes like the rest of the teenagers.

Becky was eager to let Tom get out of their apartment after being cooped-up all day because of the snowstorm. She even let him take the car, warning him to drive careful, and making sure he was dressed warm enough. Blue jeans, a couple of sweaters over a shirt, two pairs of gloves, two pairs of wool socks, earmuffs, stocking cap, varsity jacket, and snow boots. Tom thought, "Enough clothes to keep anybody warm, even a seventeen year old, and still you had to look cool."

Outside, it took a good half hour to uncover the car from the fresh snow and make a path to the road for the '57 Chevy to get out. The trip to Dad's took a half hour, and the toboggan was lashed to the top of the car. Tom was off to meet the guys. The new snow tires really helped the car handle well in the fresh snow. Tom could hear the crunch under the tires and remembered thinking the packing was going to be excellent for making a toboggan run.

Terry's mom greeted him at the front door just like a mother hen. She was double-checking to make sure Tom was dressed warm enough, offering an extra scarf or some more gloves, maybe. Mrs. Schram was always looking out for all of the boys. There, Tom met Rob Thompson, Tim Wilk, Ron Klein, and Larry Parker.

Terry Schram was a nice Baptist boy. He was always full of life and never seemed to have a moody streak. He was very popular with the guys and the girls in school.

Rob Thompson was always a leader when it came to partying or just cruising around in his 1949 Mercury. Tom remembers the time Rob asked him to paint something on the back quarter panel of his '49 Merc. That was the in thing to do in the 60's. So, Tom painted a pair of dice suspended with a white cord representing "Paradise". Rob was always very proud of the logo and could be found in front of flashing blue lights of the local police car on a Saturday night.

Tim Wilk was a really fast, good-looking, Polish boy. He lived with just his mother but was always running with Rob. They lived very close to each other and naturally were best friends. Tim got into a fight one time at the Clover Bowling Alley with a guy twice his size. In the end Tim was so quick the guy was slapped to death, and exhausted, he apologized to Tim.

Ron Klein was a tag-along. He was always eager to join in, but was always looking for approval. He was loyal and often humorous with unexpected comments. But, really Ron was a good guy and friend to Tom.

Larry Parker was one of the best looking guys in the class. He was known as the best dancer, and the girls always sought him out on the dance floor. He was not an athlete though of spirit or conviction.

What a crew, and Tom knew they were going to have a blast, but little did he know how much these guys would mean to him.

They all piled into the '57 Chevy with the usual arguing over who would get to ride shotgun (next to the window). Next the insults started flying back and forth over the origin of one's birth or the occupation of one's mother. They all knew this was just kidding around, and no one meant anything they said seriously. This was supposed to be cool, and if you could outdo the other guys line, a response of ooohs, aaahs, and laughter was heard from all the others. Then there was the old habit of hearing a fart or the imitation of one expelling gas, and the culprit it was blamed on would have to yell, "safetys!" Or else, he would get a slug on the arm from the others for not saying it quick enough. It sounds dumb, but you had to play these games in order to be with the crowd back in those days.

The roads were in pretty good shape considering how much snow had fallen. The slush left by the plows and salt trucks made it just right for cruising at the regular speed limit.

Tom wasted no time heading for Clover Park, where they had all discussed trying to shoot the creek. Shooting the creek meant getting your toboggan down the hill, avoiding the few pine trees at the bottom, so it will fly over the creek. If you failed to do so, it meant sudden disaster, as you would spill out into a possible wet creek bottom. But, tonight with the weather so cold, the creek would surely be frozen over. Still, the skill it took to avoid the trees and clear the span of the creek was a challenge

The full moon made the evening even more exciting. Believe it or not, they didn't even have any booze with them and everyone was looking forward to a good time. The subject of beer wasn't even discussed to Tom's surprise. They were all just looking forward to getting there before anyone else had touched the hills or ruined the first runs. To their amazement there wasn't a soul at the park probably because it was after 11:00 p.m. before they arrived. Pretty late for a bunch of teenagers to be out, but then there was no school tomorrow.

They scrambled out of the car and dislodged the toboggan from the top of the car. Tom's father had waxed the toboggan before they picked it up. It was very slippery on the new snow as it started to slide away. Chasing the sled, Terry Schram caught on the first try and lined it up on top of the hill for the first run. The first run was being prepared, and they took considerable effort to make sure everyone had their legs and arms interlocked. The procedure was performed at the beginning of each and every run to ensure a successful run.

The first person on the sled would sit down as close to the curved front of the toboggan, locking his legs so the heels of his boots fit between the curved front and in between the front edge of the sled and the chains that held the curved portion to the flat seating portion. This enabled the first rider to steer the toboggan by pressing his right foot forward or his left foot forward. The second rider sat behind the first, wrapping his legs over onto the first rider's lap. Each leg was held in place by the front man holding his arms over the legs and pulling the legs in to his body. Each rider would scoot forward so as to leave enough room on the back for another. The eight-foot toboggan would easily handle all six of them. The last rider was assigned the job of pushing them off on a run and jumping aboard to take his position the same as the rest of them.

It was the duty of the first rider to yell the commands for steering this vehicle, or yelling to bail out if disaster was eminent. Having control over its destiny would always create a squabble over who would be first. Usually, it was a shared position, as they would rotate the honor. Sometimes, it belonged to the one who successfully completed a good run.

The last position on the toboggan was also one of equal satisfaction. It enabled the rider to have the macho image of getting the best start for the rest, but also allowed for the quickest escape. The last rider was understandably easier to extract himself from the line of entwined arms and legs.

The snow was so soft and ready for compacting. There were no marks on the hill and as far as they could tell, they were the only ones at the park. The first couple of runs were pretty slow as the snow piled up around the sled and over the top. Covered with white fluffy stuff, it created a festive romp as they all enjoyed throwing it at each other, rolling off the sled, and stuffing it into the other guy's face. They took great care in not walking up the hill in the area they wanted reserved for their runs. The first run did not even come close to the creek bed at the bottom. As the night progressed the snow packed, the runs began to get longer, and the creek was getting closer to the end of our runs. Finally, they had formed a pretty compact run, and they were sure they could shoot the creek.

The first attempt was a dumper as they entered the creek bed and found the ice solid enough to hold all their weight. The temperature was cold enough; they weren't going to get wet tonight. A few more runs and they were making the other side of the creek with ease. Much to their displeasure though, they were not flying over the creek and had given up trying to be airborne.

It was getting past midnight and the runs were getting routine. For some reason Tom had wandered down the hill to the north and found what appeared to be a natural toboggan run built into the side of the same hill they were using. Tom let out a yell, and they all came down to see what it was he was so excited about.

Smooth as silk from the first fallen snow, it glistened from the moon glowing on it like a bobsled run at the Olympics. A half-tube curving slightly to the south and then opening to the bottom of the hill and running parallel with the creek. There were no trees in the path as it doglegged past the standing pines that were across the hill at the bottom.

"Man, we can go forever! Nothing in our way! The creek won't stop us! Nothing will!" Tom exclaimed with frost coming from his breath, as the night was getting colder now.

They were all very excited, and the anxious arguments for positions started.

Finally, they had come to a resolution. The toboggan was Tom's, so Tom claimed his rightful position as first seat. Besides, Tom's old football instinct would not let anybody else volunteer before him when it came to some sort of possible challenge. Second seat went to Rob Thompson, third seat to Terry Schram, fourth seat to Ron Klein, fifth seat to Larry Parker, and last to the most macho, Tim Wilk.

They all sensed this might be the last run because they were all getting cold and tired. They wanted to make it the best run of all.

They felt the landscape was perfect, and the snow had become hardened for packing with the cold temperature. The moon was shining over the hillside, lighting the entire path for the tremendous event that we hoped was to be experienced. Each helped the other to lock-in because their future run into the record books was before them.

Tim Wilk gave a yell, "GO WILDCATS!" as he took his long strides toward the hill. He jumped aboard and locked his legs over the man in front of him.

Tom remembered the traditional cry for the start of the football game and was proud that Tim had remembered it also.

There they were sailing down the shoot, as smart and fast as though they were on a bobsled at the Olympic games. The speed was faster than they had experienced all night. Snow was flying past them on both sides of the toboggan, like a rooster tail of water behind a speedboat. They were all yelling at the top of their lungs, and they had not reached top speed yet. It was at the bottom, as the hill started around and out to a level plain area where Tom could barely recall seeing a small black spot on the surface of the snow in front of the toboggan.

Thump . . . crack . . . ugh . . . and then everything went black. When Tom came to, all he could see was the big full bright moon shining down on him. The ground was cold and Tom's head was aching fiercely, as well as his chest and midsection. Damn it was cold. Then Tom felt the pain racing throughout his body. Tom tried to move his legs, and the pain shot through him again.

'My God, what had happened,' Tom thought.

The next thing Tom remembered Terry Schram was leaning over him and holding his hand.

"Tom, just lay still. Don't try to move." Terry said.

The toboggan had hit a pipe, covered by the fresh fallen snow. The top of the pipe had penetrated Tom's chest, but thank God, he had put on all those shirts, and Varsity jacket. There was blood but not much as the material was soaking most of it up. The top of the pipe had cracked through the center of the toboggan breaking the first and second cross bars and split the centerboard clean through the length of the sled. Tom was the first on the sled but the last remaining body to stay on the toboggan having the pipe split his pelvic bone, and the tip of the pipe broke his sternum.

The toboggan on impact catapulted the others over Tom's head and sprayed their bodies on the bottom of the hill. Rob Thompson landed on his shoulder and was feeling O.K. Terry Schram said he landed on top of Rob but was all right. Ron Klein landed face first next to a tree that he just missed hitting and was just shaken. Larry Parker had wrenched his knee, but was limping a little. Tim Wilk stayed on his feet, but ended up passing by the creek. It looked like; overall, Tom had collected all the damages. The guys rallied around, each taking off their jackets to keep Tom warm, offering Tom their gloves, asking how they could help, and trying to collect themselves into some kind of rescue team.

Finally, Tim Wilk asked Jerry to try and get Tom's car keys from his pocket. Terry was very concerned as Tom grimaced with pain as he retrieved the keys. Tim decided to take Rob and Larry with him to try and get help. An ambulance was needed, and the town was dead asleep. Tom later found out they tried running red lights, banged on doors, and called an operator on a payphone and finally got help. They were sure Tom wasn't going to make it, and at that very moment Tom thought so too.

Terry Schram, the guy with all the right things to say at the right time and with a sense of humor stayed by Tom's side. Terry kept trying to make Tom more comfortable without moving him. Asking Ron Klein for coat or scarf or anything to keep Tom from getting cold. Terry would prop Tom's head up and then lower it for him. He was constantly chattering to Tom, as he seemed to be going in and out of consciousness. Ron was standing off to the side, and Tom could tell by his expression that he was pretty worried also. The pain was constant and progressively worse and Tom tried but couldn't stop the tears.

Tom was thinking of all the football players he had tackled or hit in his past four years on the football field and in practice. There wasn't anything as hard as that pipe. Even that 300-pound fullback from Southville High, and even line of blockers in the Meat Grinder did not feel as hard as hitting that pipe.

Finally, Tom had met his match and this stinking little one-inch pipe had ripped him in two. The time seemed to be slowing down, and Tom was wondering if there was ever going to be anything else but this continual pain from inside his body.

Now, Tom started thinking of dieing, and the thought was not that scary. At least the pain would be over.

"Terry," Tom said, "Am I going to die? Please God, make the pain stop!"

Terry tried to reassure Tom that everything was going to be all right. At the same time he was yelling, "Where the hell are those guys? What could be taking so long?"

Then he started getting Tom to take his mind off the pain.

First thing in Terry's mind, "What about those girls? Which one you like the best? Out of all the girls in our class, Tom, which one did you like the best?"

The only name that came to Tom's mind Christine Baker, and Tom knew Terry and Larry Landon were battling it out for her favor. Tom didn't know why he said her name, and he thought it was funny that it was Terry who just happened to be there.

Tom said, "I didn't do right by her back in the summer before our junior year, but I think things would have been a lot different if I had."

"She's O.K.," Terry said.

Then came a confession from Tom, "Oh, God, if I die now, I'll have died a virgin. Oh, I wished I had treated Christine better. I think she was the only girl I ever cared about." Tom was weeping now and shaking nervously, partly from the cold and partly from fear.

Tom didn't think Terry was too keen on hearing all about his feeling for his girl, and he immediately tried to get him on another subject.

"Tom, tell me something. What ever made you play football the way you did?" Terry asked.

"What do you mean? I loved the game!" Tom answered.

"Yes, but you should have never been on the field at 107-pounds!" he said, "You played like a vengeance or that you didn't care what ever happened to you, like there was no tomorrow. Why did you play like that? Tell me, I could never figure you out. Everyone wanted to play like you, but couldn't find the nerve or the will power to do the things you did?"

"Terry, I don't think I'm going to make it! I don't think I'm going to get my first girl. Promise me, you will tell Christine what I said" Tom gasped and paused because he needed to take some deep breaths to stay conscious.

"Terry, I think I'm going to tell you what I have been carrying around inside of me for the last two years. The burdensome secret that made me want to play the game of football. The reason I tried to hit so hard, play so much, and do what no one else wanted to do. I don't think I'll be seeing the light of morning anyway." Tom thought he wasn't ever going to leave the bottom of that hill.

Just then a paramedic was opening Tom's shirt and asking Tom where it hurt the most. Before long he was on a stretcher and heading up the hill to an ambulance and the hospital.

If you have a wounded heart,
Touch it as little as you would
An injured eye.
There are only two remedies
For the suffering of the soul:
Hope and Patience
Pythagoras

CHAPTER 10

HOW TOM ROONEY GOT TOUGH

Tom Rooney was born the fifth and last child of Becky and Gus Rooney. Becky was of Scottish and Irish heritage, and Gus was of Irish descendants. They started their marriage early as they ran away to Indiana so Becky, just 15 years old, would not need marital consent from her parents. Gus was 21 years old, and they started having kids with Becky only 22 years old when Tom was born.

The family grew fast and furious with Gary born first, then Darren and Danny, followed by Marsha, and then Tom. Tom being the youngest had special privileges for sometime as a toddler. He was always carried around and attended to by his older brothers and sister, even though she was just two years older. This was necessary as Gus was drafted into the Army during World War II, one month after Becky gave birth to Tom.

Tom's grandparents on Becky's side came to their daughters rescue as she was left with five children, ten chickens, one roster, a milk cow, and a Shetland pony all on 10 acres of land called a farm. Grandma and Grandpa loaded them all into their old Plymouth and settled them down in Macon, Georgia to grow a Victory Garden to survive.

Two years later Gus returned from Italy with a purple heart, bronze star, and a full discharge. He took one look at his family and let them know they didn't belong in Georgia and hauled them all back to Michigan where they would be close to his family.

Gus Rooney came back from the war a different man than Becky had known when they were so deeply in love as young people. Gus had a drive to go to work and support his family. He moved them back to the farm, but soon moved into town closer to his work. Gus had also acquired an Irish temper, and, unfortunately, Tom would have to witness it almost every day of his life.

Tom's toddler years were marked by two serious episodes that could have killed most babies, but Tom was a survivor. First, he had drunk some kerosene left in a jar by the back door to be used for a lantern in the barn. As Tom began to turn blue and started passing out, Becky rushed him to the nearest hospital. The nurses at the hospital stuck Tom in a room with some other children and told Becky he would be fine by morning. Luckily, Becky's sister arrived. Aunt Betty scooped up baby Tom and rushed him over to the Methodist Hospital where they immediately pumped his stomach and saved Tom. Second, he was so curious over his new home in the city, Tom just had to have a better look out the upstairs window. So, Tom crawled out of his crib onto the windowsill, pushed the screen out, and fell down two stories. A construction crew was putting in a footing for the home next store, and as they came around the corner pouring their concrete someone yelled, "Hey there's a kid down here playing in the dirt, stop the concrete!" Needless to say they didn't need Tom Rooney's help.

Marsha and Tom were always very close. Marsha was always a big help to Becky, changing diapers, getting new bottles of milk, or putting a bandage on all the trouble Tom could find to get into. Marsha and Tom also shared the childhood diseases together such as measles, mumps, chicken pox, and tonsillitis. Tom can still remember when his sister and he shared a hospital room and brought all the wheelchairs into the room in the middle of the night. All hell broke loose the next morning when the hospital staff tried to open the door into the room so they could prepare them for their tonsillectomy. Tom was laughing all the way down to surgery until the anesthesia took hold.

Before Tom was five years old his older brothers loved to play tricks on Tom. The old term, "double dog dare you" was echoed through out the home. When Becky was down in the basement washing clothes in the old wringer washing machine or hanging clothes outside on the clotheslines, or shopping with Marsha, it would provide a perfect time for the boys to be in charge of Tom.

Gary, Darren, and Danny would conjure up the strangest and most horrible recipes for their little naïve brother Tom. A typical blend would be Cheerios cereal covered with molasses, ketchup, mustard, salt, pepper, with chili powder for flavoring, all served up in a bowl of milk. As they all gathered around the oak table in the kitchen with Tom sitting up high on his booster chair, his guardians would all start chanting, "Double dog dare you to eat it, Tom!"

Tom would eat it thinking he was gaining their respect and admiration, and he had built himself a reputation of never turning down a dare, especially a double dog dare! Later he would suffer terrible stomach cramps, headaches, or multiple trips to the john with diarrhea or vomiting. Becky would never understand why her little Tommy was sick so often.

Tom was the scrawny one of the four boys, so it was normal for them to chase Tom and get him down on the ground or floor for a good scrubbing of his head with their knuckles or pinching him or tickling him till he urinated or swore.

Now, this would go on whenever their mom was not at home. Tom learned the only way to get them to stop was to let out a litany of screams culminated by a few choice swear words he had collected in his vocabulary while eavesdropping on Becky and Gus arguing. Then the boys would race to meet their mother at the door when she came home to report what Tom had said in front of all of them, failing to mention why or for what reason. Tom grew up with the taste of either Life Boy or Ivory bar soap for a cure to his addiction of swearing.

One time, Danny had jumped on Tom and was torturing him until Tom slipped away, and as he stomped up the stairs yelling all the profanity he could muster, Tom stopped at the top of the stairs and turned around saying, "You go ahead and tell mom, I don't care!"

Then Tom picked up his cap gun that was laying on the lid to the laundry shoot on top of the stairs and threw it at Danny breaking Danny's arm and rewarding Tom with another bar of Life Boy mouthwash and a couple of lashes from his fathers belt.

Tom was to endure all of this and was still not able to get his brothers approval. But, the last humiliation came when Tom started kindergarten at the age of five. Michigan winters were bitter cold and on this particular morning the frost was everywhere.

The whole gang would always gather at the end of the driveway next to the metal mailbox mounted on a steel pole. Tom's brothers would always be throwing snow on the girls or washing their little brothers face with a snowball. Darren started really getting to Tom, and Tom had just about had enough. Finally, Darren said, "You are not going to cry are you. Why don't you stick your tongue on the mailbox post, and you won't cry." The rest of the guys caught on right away and started chanting double dog dare you!

Tom still hadn't grown out of taking a dare, and he knew if he would do this they would stop picking on him. So, after the third or fourth double dog dare, Tom did the unthinkable. As the bus arrived, Tom could be heard screaming at the top of his lungs even though obstructed by his frozen tongue, for his Mom! Excruciating pain and hysterical laughter filled the air as the busload of school kids watched Tom out of the bus windows. The driver of the bus saw what was happening and ran to the house and banged on the door. Becky answered and came running with hot water from the tea-kettle to rescue her little Tommy.

Tom would always remember this incident in his life and screaming and moaning as he repeated every swear word he could think of in his vocabulary. This time no soap, just hot chocolate, and Tom got to stay home from school the whole day.

Tom had become pretty tough by his ordeals with his brothers, but couldn't grow as fast as he wanted. Always, Tom's brothers told Tom that he was so small and not big like them because he was probably adopted, and maybe someday they would give him back. Tom remembers going to see their family doctor and broke out in tears because he was so small. He showed the doctor how he could stretch his two hands around his waist and said this is not healthy. The doc laughed at Tom and said, "Son, some day you will be going to a doctor to lose weight.

Tom had escaped his brother's torture twice in his memory. Once was when they chased him upstairs and he made it inside the bathroom. Tom's uncle had built the house and must have had Tom in mind as he installed the bathroom toilet right behind the door to the bathroom. Tom

sat on the john and held his feet on the back of the door, so the brothers couldn't get him. Tom thought his mom would never get home.

The second time, Tom ran up the stairs and was terrified to the extent that he went into his sister's bedroom, opened the window, removed the screen, and jumped out the second story window. The brothers couldn't believe Tom had gone that far to escape their torture. But, they forgot that Tom had experience and hit the ground and rolled just like he did when he was a toddler.

Tom had been made tough by his ordeals with his father as well. Gus had come from a stern very disciplined Irish family receiving many beatings by his father. Tom received more than his share from a razor strap his father had hanging in the basement or from the belt his father wore and was always very dramatic as he took it from the belt loops on his pants and then applied it to Tom's behind. Once, when Tom was told to go to the basement to receive his punishment, he tried to hide a magazine in his britches. As the belt hit its intended target, Gus was not fooled. Tom was ordered to take off all his clothes.

Two days of school were missed, and Becky put Vaseline on his scars until they were not noticeable.

Tom avoided a beating one time when he was sent to the basement, as his father was about to administer the punishment for saying the "f" word for the first time in his young life, Becky again came to the rescue. She wanted to know where he had heard such language, and it certainly was not in this house. Tom told them that he heard them last night having one of their disagreements and they had used the word. They both thought it over, and Tom got a bar of Life Boy, instead.

Tom still idolized his brothers and always wanted to be like them. They all played football, and Tom tried desperately to keep up with them in anything they would do in school. Danny played the drums, so Tom tried for a while to play them. Gary was on an Oakbrook football team that was never scored against, and Tom was the team manager. Darren played all the sports and Tom was to follow the best he could as they had prepared him to be tough.

If man is moderate and contended,
Then even age is no burden;
If he is not, then even youth is full of cares.
Plato

CHAPTER 11

HOSPITAL 101

The paramedic was kneeling beside him as he asked Tom for his name. He was opening his box of magic and unzipping a duffle bag as his assistants scrambled around unwrapping a thermo blanket.

First the medic said, "Tom, where does it hurt?"

Tom replied, "Mostly my pelvic area, and both my hips are killing me. My chest is hurting also."

"O.K.," he replied, "we'll get right on it. You just try and lay perfectly still, and we'll get you off this hill."

The medical people started talking about vital signs, feeling a pulse, eyes, and most of it was a pretty fuzzy to Tom as he would close his eyes and just try not to move. Tom remembers the thermo blanket being wrapped around him, but as soon as they tried to move him his pain was unbearable and Tom screamed.

"O.K., this is the situation. We will put the board under you without moving you. The snow is deep enough, we will be able to slide it all the way underneath him while you all stabilize his body," he explained to everyone.

Before long Tom was being carried up the hill by a band of rescuers and placed on a gurney waiting behind an ambulance. They rolled the gurney inside the vehicle being very careful not to let Tom move. Tom felt a little warmer now that he was inside the ambulance. But, the medics started an IV as Tom just stayed still trying not to move and cause the pain to start all over again.

Terry Schram said to the ambulance personnel, "We will go get Tom's mom and meet you at the hospital. It's the Methodist Hospital, is that right?"

The next thing Tom remembers was being examined in the emergency room. Several nurses and doctors were hovering over him and were busy trying to remove his clothing. They were being very careful with Tom's legs and trying not to move them or his hips. The chest injury was not too serious, but still they cut all those shirts off with scissors and started to cut the pants, which were really nice Levi's. When they got to the boots, they handled them with kid gloves, and Tom didn't feel a thing. Tom saw his Varsity jacket hanging on a hook on the wall and thought, thank God, they didn't damage or cut it.

Doctors were conferring and decided the next step should be X-rays, but they were uncomfortable about transporting him any further so they ordered the portable unit to be brought to the examining room. Many different angles were shot, and Tom was put to sleep with some medication. As Tom dosed off he thought he probably would make it with all this care.

Tom woke up to a bright sunny room and he was warm even though he felt just a clean sheet against his body and a light blanket covered his bed. The bed was beside some windows. Tom noticed the frost covered windowpanes with their frozen snowflake designs around the corners and clear holes in the center of each one. It was definitely cold outside, and Tom was glad he was nice and warm inside.

A curtain surrounded two sides of his bed, and he could hear people talking on the other side. Finally, Tom thought he heard his Mom's voice, and then he heard someone say her name, Becky. Tom said, "Mom is that you out there?"

"Well look who's awake," the doctor said as he pulled the curtain back handing it to a nurse that pushed it toward the wall at the headboard. Dr. Morris, the old family doctor that had delivered most of Becky's children stood there with his clipboard, arms folded over his chest, and pen in his hand said, "Got someone here, who is anxious to see you, Tom."

Tom's mother stepped up to the bed with tears in her eyes wiping them with handkerchief and reached to give Tom a hug but being careful not to move him. Then Tom said, "Mom, it's O.K. Mom, I'll be fine, don't cry." Tom said, "What's all this strapping across the bed for Doc? I'm not going anywhere?"

Becky started to explain to Tom, but Dr. Morris interrupted her to explain exactly to Tom how much damage was done to his body on that last run.

Dr. Morris explained, "Tom, you injured your spleen slightly, and we are going to monitor that. You have a pelvic bone that has been split like a V-shape and you have cracked both hips up the sides."

"Oh, is that all!" Tom said.

"Well son, we are going to put you back together by putting you in traction to pull your leg bones out of the hip sockets and hopefully everything will settle back in place and heal properly. Tom, it is going to be a very long time, and it will take a lot of your courage and cooperation to assist in this healing process. You will not be getting out of bed and you will have to use a bedpan," Dr. Morris explained.

Tom said, "How long, Doc? Will I be out in time to try out for the basketball team this year?

"No Tom, we don't think you will be playing any basketball, or baseball this spring," Dr. Morris was quite serious. "We are not sure how long this will take because this is a first for all of us around here. Truthfully, we can't promise you at this time that you will ever walk again."

Tom was silent for a moment while Becky started to cry again. Then Tom said, "Come on Mom, look at the bright side, I'll be out of your hair for awhile, and you won't have to worry about me. I won't be going out and getting into any more trouble, for awhile anyway." Tom was covering up for his disappointment, but didn't want his mom to worry. "Hey, what's the food like around this place? Any breakfast available?" Tom said trying to cheer everybody up.

First, the mechanical engineers came in to rig up the cables, springs, and bars to assemble the traction apparatus. Tom was to be chained to this contraption for the rest of his senior year. Then as he was provided a trapeze bar in front of his face, a nice candy striper came in with a full breakfast with eggs, bacon, and potatoes. Juice and fruit was also provided, and she left a menu for lunch and dinner as well as tomorrows selection as well. Tom was to fill out a lot of these over the year.

Tom had a good appetite but could feel the slight pain in his chest and pelvis area and tried very hard not to move around in the bed. This in time became very boring and was very uncomfortable for a seventeen-year-old young man. Tom hated to think of the first time he had to use a bedpan. Then when the time came, Tom endured the pain necessary to be moved onto this thing underneath him. Future trips became easier, but still very immodest to say the least. Having others to help you and clean up after you was not anything anyone wants to get used to but was necessary. Tom had never felt so helpless, but was always very humbled and grateful for all their attention.

So this was to be Tom's senior year. He would have a lot of time to meditate, study, and think about his future. Meditate, he did a lot about the situation he had put himself into over the junior and senior year of football and change in personality and mindset that had burdened him because of his past. His home life sucked, his relationship with his Father sucked, and his outlook on his future was not good. Tom would have six months to contemplate and correct all these problems by himself.

Tom began to plan on his studies and had someone bring his homework to the hospital. It was only early November, and Tom didn't want to fall behind in his schoolwork. Tom had always been pretty good with his grades in high school. Back in the ninth grade he had even thought of wanting to go to West Point. He had researched the possibilities, but then he received his first C in a science class. He studied aggressively for that class and had to settle with a C+, so West Point was out of the question now. His grade point going into his senior year was a B, but now he would have to make the grades all by himself.

Tom liked his class on U.S. Government, required by all seniors, most of all and kept up to date on all the material and homework. The math class came easy, as he liked Algebra. The typing class suffered the most because he couldn't do the typing while in his hospital bed. The final class was shop class, and all he had to do is wait for the final exam and study wood types, finishes, glues, and shop tool identifications.

As for Tom's future he started to think about going to college but knew he would have to come up with a plan to achieve this goal by himself. Tom knew he couldn't count on his parents in their situation. He started asking questions of the many patients who came and went from his six-bed ward about their experiences and how he might get to college. The military seemed to be the best solution. But as Tom lay there in his hospital bed with all the physical damage to his body, this option was not promising.

After the first couple of weeks, things in Tom's hospital room got down to a regular routine. Tom had a television and a telephone that he was able to use. He liked Bonanza and watched a lot of Dragnet and the local news broadcasts. The telephone could only make long distance calls. Tom didn't make many, but would receive calls from his Mom or Dad once in awhile.

The third week brought forth boredom and depression. Lying in the same position day after day, night after night was getting old. The staff was worrying about Tom getting bedsores so they frequently were changing his bedding or making changes to his mattress to make sure the sores never appeared. Each evening after dinner a very tall, beautiful black girl named Allison would come into the room and move from bed to bed offering back rubs. She would apply lotions to the patients' back and with those long black fingers, give each and everyone of them a wonderful massage. All except, Tom. She would stop by Tom's bed and talk to him and tell him someday she is going to give him his first back rub, and Tom would always get very excited as any seventeen-year old young man would.

One day when Tom was feeling really down and depression was creeping up on him again, Coach Ford stormed into Tom's room. He had a projector and a movie screen he immediately assembled at the foot of Tom's bed. The other patients in the room didn't quite know what to make of this man. He was so boastful and commanding and took over the room. He said, "Hey Rooney, wait to see what I got on this film!"

While he was busy putting everything together and talking continuously about how the guys from the old football team sent their regards, but were sorry they couldn't be there. Tomorrow was the Senior Skip Day, and he was going to try and make it up for Tom not being able to attend. He presented Tom with a card that the team had all signed individually, and then Coach Ford invited all the other patients to join them to watch, "The gutless wonder in action!"

The film was of the game against Southville with their 300-pound fullback. The one play Coach Ford played over and over was the one where Southville was on their two-yard line, and they handed off to their fullback. He hit the line just as you could see Rooney come up from his safety position and hit the big guy head on in his stomach and drove him back into the end zone. The officials came running up to the play and put the ball on the one-yard line, and said it was fourth down. Tom was escorted off the field to replace a broken helmet and get some smelling salts to clear the cobwebs away and release the butterflies he was seeing.

The patients in the ward didn't really understand what was going on except for one or two who liked football. Some had just come back from surgery and were not so comfortable with Coach's visit. Soon, some nurses came down from their nurse's station and asked Coach to stop the film and let the patients have some quiet rest after their operations. Someone had pushed their call button and ended Coach's finest hour.

Coach Ford left and really picked Tom up from having a bummer of a day. Senior Skip Day was always looked forward to, as the seniors were able to miss school and go ice-skating and tobogganing. Needless to say, Tom wasn't going to miss the latter. The patients had to know who Coach Ford was, and they knew how much Tom was surprised by his presents. They could tell he was a man Tom really respected and worshipped.

A month had passed, and Tom was really getting antsy with the lack of motion and the weights pulling on his legs were getting heavier and heavier.

The bedpan was literally a pain in the ass, but was regrettably necessary. Tom tried everything to pass the time by playing solitaire, checkers, and even throwing cards into his bedpan that one of the other patients set up for him. The nurses didn't like picking up all the missed shots. He tried very hard not to ask for help or use his call button except at night when he couldn't sleep because of pain or headaches.

Tom's birthday was fast approaching, and he was getting pretty depressed over having to spend his eighteenth birthday in the hospital. The day came and the staff tried to cheer him up right away with a cupcake on his breakfast tray and a lit candle. They all stepped into the ward to sing happy birthday to him asking the other patients to join in. The only thing Tom could think of when they asked him to blow out the candle was wishing he could get out of this bed.

It was almost seven o'clock in the evening when Tom saw Terry Schram at the door of his ward. He said to keep it quiet that he had a surprise for Tom. He left and came right back in with two or three classmates as he shuffled back and forth from the hallway to the room he was opening a stairwell door to let more and more classmates into the room. This is how they were getting on the floor without going past the nurse's station after visiting hours. With just four of the beds being occupied by patients, they were just as surprised as Tom and didn't seem to mind the assault.

Rob Thompson, Ron Klein, and Janet Toth were the first invaders. Rob and Ron set out stringing rolls of crate paper, Tom's favorite colors, blue and white of Oakville High. The strands hung from curtain rods on one side of the room to the other side, from hospital bed to another and soon the room was covered with streamers.

Larry Landon and Christine Baker were next and they set about taking a banner over the windows proclaiming, HAPPY 18TH BIRTHDAY!!!!

Tim Wilk and Loni Parker came in next and started hanging some kind of curtain to cover the curtain surrounding the bed. After they were done they closed the curtain and covered the bed with a bedspread full of teddy bears.

Janet Toth was busy taping rabbit fur to my bedpan and walked over to the end of the bed and picked up the weights holding Tom's legs out of his hip sockets and asked, "What are these things for?" as she lifted them in the air and let them drop. Tom was so surprised by all the activity he didn't even noticed the sudden jerked reaction he was having.

Dan Cracker, John Stokes, Johny Street, and Doug Betters came in with a birthday cake, inflated balloons, and soda. Christine was busy lighting the eighteen candles when everyone started singing happy birthday to Tom.

Ron Klein was looking over the doctor's clipboard at the end of the bed.

Tom made the same wish as he did in the morning and blew out all the candles. His friends started pulling out all the candles and cutting the cake to serve to everyone including the patients at the other beds first. Sodas were being distributed to everyone just as a nurse came in and said, "What is going on?"

Then the floor supervisor came in and exclaimed, "Why weren't we invited?"

So the party continued and the hospital staff was wonderful, as they knew how this would help Tom's depression. The patients were grateful because Tom's friends included them, and the guys couldn't take their eyes off Christine and Janet.

The supervisor let the party go on for about a half hour and then asked everyone to help clean up the crate paper, but let them keep the bedspread and banner on the window for now. She didn't notice the shower curtain with the pinup girls until she went to close it and was shocked over the bedpan decoration. It wasn't until the next morning when the doctor came by to visit Tom, the Playboy centerfold was found. They all got a laugh out of it.

Before they left each one of them came to Tom's bedside to give him a hug and wish him happy birthday again. Tom was holding back the tears as they all left, and the room became very quiet again. Tom didn't need any sleeping pills or pain pills as he slept very well that night knowing he was now eighteen years old and not forgotten by his friends at school.

Months came and went and an endless stream of patients came and went from the hospital ward where Tom was residing. So many he could not remember all of them. Two stuck in his mind though. A man came in to have the bed next to Tom. Tom knew he was in a lot of pain as he was always using the call button. The nurses would make him more comfortable by adjusting his bed or giving him some pain medication. Then one day when Tom woke up the man was gone. The nurse said he had gone down for surgery. Later that day, the man returned and was still recovering from the anesthesia. It wasn't until late in the evening he spoke to Tom and said he was really feeling better. Tom had to ask, "What kind of surgery did you have?"

The man answered, "I had a tonsillectomy and hemorrhoids removed."

Tom just started to laugh because it was the greatest thing he had heard all month.

The second patient he remembered came into the hospital ward during the night. It was a terrible commotion that woke him from his sleep. The man was being moved to the bed beside the windows across from Tom. Tom heard him moaning over and over, "I can't believe she shot me!"

The next morning the man's wife came in yelling, "I'll shoot you again, if I ever catch you messing' around with my sister again! You miserable husband." At least they kept it in the family.

Throughout the hospital stay Tom had family members visit him, but not too often as his brothers and sister were working on their careers and must have been very busy. Tom's one brother, Darren, had entered the army and was stationed in Germany. Gary was going to General Motors Institute and working in the factory. His sister, Marsha was working for a loan office and trying to take some secretarial classes at a local college. Becky was in and out frequently, but Tom's Father came just one time. That was O.K. with Tom.

By the time the sixth month came around that Tom had been in the hospital, he was beginning to wonder if he would graduate with his classmates. Finally, word came from the school that Tom had passed his exams that he completed right there in the hospital. He would graduate with the class and be awarded a diploma even if he couldn't attend the ceremony.

Tom was determined more than ever to attend the graduation and kept asking the nurses to talk to the doctors to get their latest results of his stay in their fine facility. Finally, one day Dr. Morris came in the room with a couple of nurses and explained. He wanted Tom to sit up on the edge of his bed at least twice a day for the next week. Tom asked when they would be removing the traction apparatus. Doc said before he would leave the room.

Tom could hardly wait, as he was very anxious to get started. That night he sat on the bedpan on the side of the bed dangling his feet over the side. The next morning he was asking the nurses to let him dangle some more and kept his schedule until next week.

The next Monday, Doc arrived and said, "Let's get this young man on his feet today." The nurses pulled his bedspread down to the end of the bed and got on the side of the bed. First, they swung Tom's legs off the edge of the bed, and each one held Tom's arms and forearm as they moved Tom forward and placed his slippers on the floor. Tom was so confident he could stand, he said, "Let go. Let go!" Then he almost collapsed on the floor before they caught him.

"Not so fast, Tom," the Doc said, "We have a week of rehabilitation so you can use crutches before I let you get out of here."

Right to the end the hospital staff gave Tom all the attention he needed. One evening Allison stopped by his bed and said, "Tom, are you ready for that back rub I promised you?"

Tom was in seventh heaven and enjoyed every stroke from those long beautiful fingers.

So, Tom did what he was told for the next week and on Friday they wheeled him to the entrance of the hospital, handed him his crutches, and waved goodbye.

Six months and seven days had passed before Tom walked back into Oakbrook High school. The day was spent saying hello and goodbye to all his teachers, coaches, and classmates.

Right to the end Tom's classmates were being very attentive to him. They were all gathered at the railing overlooking the gymnasium and the guys were trying out Tom's crutches. Them Tom asked for them and found that the guys had put them in the janitor's trash barrel on wheels and sent it into the girls-restroom. To Tom's surprise, Christine and Janet went in and retrieved them for him.

Tom attended the graduation ceremony practice that evening and found out he was to be one of the last ones to receive their diploma because of his crutches. Tom didn't mind as he had reached a peace of mind during his stay in the hospital and did not feel the burdens that he had forced on himself since his junior year. Tom was ready to face his life after high school. Before the year was out, Tom found himself enlisted in the U. S. Army to see the world.

It is not good for all your wishes to be fulfilled:
Through sickness you recognize the value of health,
Through evil the value of god,
Through hunger satisfaction,
Through exertion the value of rest.
Heraclitus

CHAPTER 12

TOM ROONEY'S BURDEN

It had often been written and said the 60's were a turbulent time. The town of Oakbrook did not have much going on during these times. Yet, other parts of the country were having protest marches, demonstrations, or picketing for one reason or another. The residents of Oakbrook pretty much enjoyed a quite peaceful time with cool and sunny summer days. Picnics were planned, swimming or summer softball at neighboring parks and lakes. The winter months were blustery and cold with a lot of snow keeping everyone occupied with shoveling or scraping the white stuff or moving it with plows or shovels. Others spent their time inside trying to stay warm and completing a winter project of knitting or hooking a rug. Life at the Rooney house was not included in this very peaceful time.

Tom had left his sophomore year quite lonely after really messing up with the relationship he had with Christine Baker. He did not get along well with many of his friends after that, and he had become quite moody because of his home life.

His sister, Marsha had graduated from Oakbrook and had hoped to go to college. She had really good grades and would have done very well at any university. Their father, Gus didn't believe girls needed an education beyond high school, and he said he couldn't afford it anyway. Marsha was off on her senior trip with her girlfriends and other classmates. They were to visit Washington, D.C. and then go to New York City and explore Manhattan. She was gone for about a month.

When school let out, Tom didn't know what to do with himself, without a car he needed to do some work and earn a little money for spending. Besides it would get him away from the house. He went across the street from where the Rooney's lived and got a minimum wage job cutting grass, trimming trees, shrubs, and cleaning ponds and markers at the Oakbrook Park. The manager always liked the boys from across the street and had hired Tom's brother and himself many times.

When Tom was just five years old, the manager hired Tom to catch gold fish from one pond in the park and put them in another pond behind the manager's office. Tom had to keep them alive and was paid a handsome five cents per fish. This was Tom's first job and his second was killing starlings with his BB gun because they made a mess all over the park. That job did not last because the manager was going to pay Tom ten cents per bird and didn't know what a good shot Tom was. Anyway, Tom killed over a hundred starlings, picked them all up, and hauled them off to the trash.

Working at the Oakbrook Park gave Tom a lot of peace and quiet and that is what he needed. Becky and Gus were always arguing lately continuously. Tom couldn't understand how two people could be married for so long and not get along with each other. This was one of the things in the 60's not to be discussed outside of the home.

The 60's were a wonderful time for families to enjoy drive-in movies, watching television, or just enjoying life around their homes, gardens, and yard. Tom couldn't remember when his mother and father had ever done any of these things together.

Tom worried about his parents getting a divorce, but just thought it was idle talk during their rages with one another. It was certainly something that was never mentioned in public about your or any other family. In the 60's it was considered the biggest sin after the 10 commandments. No one got a divorce, at least no one that Tom ever heard about.

Tom would go up to the football field after work in the summer to get away from the house and the arguing. There he would meet some of the guys, usually older than Tom by one year and play catch with the football or run some one-on-one pass plays. Sometimes there would be enough guys for a little scrimmage. Anyway, Tom found himself being the last one picked for a side because of his small size and quiet behavior. Still the guys treated Tom like one of them and enjoyed his participation.

It was on one of these evenings Tom remembered meeting Coach Ford for the very first time. He returned home and remembered his mom had left him some leftovers because she had to go to her bowling league that night and couldn't be there to fix him a meal. Tom's father was down in the basement working. Tom yelled to him that he had returned home.

After supper Tom decided to lie on the sofa and watch a little T.V. Shortly, Tom fell off to sleep and was dreaming about maybe playing some Varsity football in the fall at the start of his junior year. Also, he had been dreaming about Christine Baker and how he could make things right with her.

Tom's mother, Becky had just stepped inside the front door and hardly had a chance to set down her bowling ball. Tom's father, Gus grabbed her by the arms and yelled, "You bitch, you whore, your nothing but a no good slut, you think I'm stupid? You don't think I know what you have been doing? You no good bitch. I've had it with you, and I'm going to teach you a lesson you'll never forget!"

The first shrill scream from his uncontrollable voice woke Tom from his restless sleep. His dad was down in the basement when Tom dosed off, and now Gus stood holding Becky tighter than Tom had ever known them to hold each other in all of his sixteen years. Gus's one hand had moved to Becky's neck, and his face was getting very red and twisted. Tom had never seen his dad in this state before, and he could hardly recognize him. But, as Tom wiped his eyes and swung his feet to the floor, sitting on the edge of the couch, he was thinking they were about to have another of their usual fights. Tom remembered the thought of maybe he had better just go to his room, but the look on Gus's face told him this was not going to be one of those ordinary fights.

Next Gus's hand left Becky's arm as he held her with the other around the neck, and her blonde hair flew wildly across her face as his fist smashed into the side of her eye.

"Mom," Tom yelled, "Dad!" But, it was too late. His mom was so shocked by the assault she didn't have any time to protect herself. Tom's dad kept up the verbal attack with language Tom had never heard either of them use against each other. He accused her of screwing everybody with long pants, and she wasn't fooling him any more. She was no good, a tramp, and had never been faithful to him ever. All this was ringing through Tom's ears, but even more through his mother's head as each word was followed by slaps and fists.

Next she was on the floor. Sobbing, trying to collect herself so to answer him but found herself shocked and speechless. Her face was marked by cuts over her eye where blood was starting to flow freely. He stood over her. Tom was on his feet about five feet away. Trembling, unbelieving, and petrified. Finally, she said, "Gus . . . . ?" And he started his assault again.

"Don't speak to me you Bitch! Don't even open that mouth of yours! I should have done this, years ago. Maybe then things would have been different!" he stammered. That's when he kicked her in the stomach. Tom's mom moaned an ungodly groan. She rolled over on her back, and her head bounced off the fireplace hearth. Gus fell on top of her with his knees straddling each side of her body. He grabbed her blonde hair, holding her by the strands through his fingers and screamed, "I'm going to treat you like I saw my father treat my mom every Saturday night at his home." Again he started his onslaught of obscenities.

Everything happened so fast, and Tom could only recall instinct taking over. He knew he had to stop his father or his mom would be dead for sure. Gus had lost all control and was beyond reason. Tom ran to them and tried to pull his dad's arm from her head. Tom could only vaguely remember Gus's arm swinging at him, and Tom found himself thrown against the wall on the other side of the living room.

Tom staggered to his feet and saw the blood pooling under his mom's head on the hearth as his father was banging her head over and over again. Tom had no other thought but to get Gus off her, and he knew he didn't have the strength to do it. Tom can't remember what drove him to his next idea but he thought, knife! Get to the kitchen and get a knife.

Tom pulled open the kitchen drawer so fast it sent all the utensils flying out on the floor. Tom saw the large carving knife his mother used on his meats and knelt down on the floor to pick it up. Tom grabbed the knife and ran to the living room. "Get off her, get off her now! Damn you, I'll cut you, if you don't get off her right now, Dad!" Tom yelled at the top of his lungs.

Gus, stopped, still sitting on top of her, and he turned to look at Tom. For a moment Tom thought he as going to call his bluff and continue his battery on his mom. Thank God, he heard Tom. He stopped and rolled off from Becky onto the floor beside her. There he sat on his ass, hands still shaking and staring at the floor.

Tom bent over his mom holding the knife toward his dad, as Gus slumped into his temporary dazed position on the floor. Tom's other hand slid under his mom's head and was immediately covered with blood. She moaned, because she was barely conscious.

"Mom! Mom, can you hear me? Mom, we have to get out of here! Mom, please!" as Tom whispered in his Mom's ear, trying to get her to come to. Tom noticed her eyes were so very blurry and rolling back into her head and the blood was covering her face as well. "Mom, come on, let's get out of here!" but Tom didn't know where to go.

Then he heard a faint voice from his mom. She could only say, "Upstairs."

Tom struggled to get her to her feet and the knife was clumsily held in his one hand trying to keep it between them and his father, but yet not worrying about the sharp edge that could have hurt them as well. Once she was erect but slumping on Tom for support, he made his way to the stairwell past his father. Staggering their way to the stairs Tom didn't know where his strength came from as his mom could hardly move. With his arm around her waist and watching the blood pour from her head onto his shirt and down her clothes onto the carpet, they finally arrived at the stairwell. Each step seemed like a giant step as Tom's mom braced herself against the railing and leaned on the wall and he on the other side taking a step at a time. Finally, reaching the top, they went down to his room and shut the door.

Once inside the room, Becky fell onto Tom's bed and the blood covered the bedspread. Her head reached the pillow as the blood still flowed from her wounds. She lay there moaning and semi-conscious as Tom tried to think of their next move. Tom listened for some sound from downstairs. First there was nothing, and then all he heard was a scream, "Damn you! Get down here, now. I'm not going to hurt you any more. You Bitch! Get down here, and I promise not to touch you."

That's when Tom first remembered starting to shake from hearing Gus's voice. Tom turned to his mom and pleaded, "Mom, what shall I do?"

She looked up holding the back of her head and faintly said, "Call police."

The phone was in the hallway between Marsha's room and Tom's. It had a very long cord so each could take it to their room for privacy. Tom was really afraid to open the door, but decided he had to so he could bring the phone to his room. If Gus were to come up the stairs, Tom didn't know if he could return to the room on time to shut the door and barricade it. Tom had no choice. He had to try or else they would be faced with an uncontrollable situation. If he could get the police, they would stop his dad. Slowly, Tom opened the door, trying not to make the slightest noise. He could hear sounds coming from the kitchen. He didn't know what Gus was doing down in the kitchen, but then panic set in as he heard the utensils on the floor being moved around. Tom thought maybe his father was looking for a knife. He got to the phone and brought it into his room. He thought now that he had the phone he didn't know what number to call. His mom faintly said, "Dial 0, Tom."

An operator answered the call, and Tom explained that he needed an ambulance and a police officer to come to the house as soon as possible. He continued to tell the operator how serious his mother's wounds looked and that she was barely conscious. The operator kept Tom on the phone until she was sure that a police officer was on his way to help them. Tom was getting very nervous about his father's moving around downstairs and not knowing what was going on down there.

Then Tom thought to tell the operator about his oldest brother, Gary. Tom didn't know his phone number, but told the operator his address as far as what street he lived on and what town the phone would be listed under. The operator assured Tom that his brother would be notified.

Then Tom heard the sound he was waiting so nervously to hear, the sound of sirens and a knocking on the front door of the house. He heard voices coming from downstairs and heard the footsteps come rushing up the steps. There was a knock on the door. As he opened it a very large size State Trooper said, "Everything is going to be alright now, son."

The officer took Tom to the other side of the room as a group of medical personnel came in and started to work on his mom. The officer was really nice and was so calming and made him feel like everything was under control now. Tom went with the officer down the stairs and out to the police cruiser to ask him some more questions. The knife was taken from him, in his room by the officer and the officer brought it to the car with them.

Tom did not see Gus as they left the house, but noticed two other police officers in the kitchen. He assumed that is where his father was but Tom didn't want to meet him anyway. Then he saw his brother Gary who wanted to know what was going on. The Police officer told him he would be with him in a moment as soon as he was finished with Tom. Then the officer said Tom could go to the hospital in the ambulance with his mom, and they would see each other again sometime in the future.

Tom saw Gary talking to the police officer and escorting him to the front door of the house. A little later the ambulance personnel brought Becky out the front door. She appeared to be covered with bandages all around her head, and they were carrying an IV bottle over her stretcher. Tom got out of the police car and entered the back of the ambulance with his mom and held her hand. She looked over at Tom and said, "Thanks, Tom."

At the hospital Tom spent the night with his mom and then was bounced around from house to house until his mom was let out of the hospital. Tom was to spend the rest of his junior and senior year sharing apartment after apartment with his mom making sure she was safe.

Tom did not see his father very often during those last years at Oakbrook and had a very bad relationship with him for many years to come.

He would never talk to anyone about that night or what really happened. When his parents were divorced, of course, it was never discussed in public or amongst friends. The burden was Tom's and his alone.

It took many years before Tom could face all of this and become the gutless wonder.

OAKBROOK HIGH
1961 FOOTBALL
SCORES

Oakbrook	30	Parkville	13
Oakbrook	0	Pearson	17
Oakbrook	27	Barkley	6
Oakbrook	13	Southville	33
Oakbrook	2	Pearson	19
Oakbrook	20	Clover	7
Oakbrook	6	Grand Bay	19
Oakbrook	21	Daniel High	33

AUTHORS EPILOGUE

Just like Tom Rooney, the author went on to
enter the military serving for three years
in Europe, traveling extensively.
This gave the author the opportunity to
enter college under the G.I. Bill and completed
a Bachelor of Science in Business.
He worked in the food service industry
and later retired as a hotel and restaurant
inspector. He has encountered many
relationships and experiences in this
field he hopes to someday publish in a book.
Later in life he became an organ donor,
giving a kidney to his sister in-law. He hopes to
tell her story as a double organ recipient,
while visiting the United States from Poland.
This is why some of the proceeds from this
Book will go to the Transplant Patient Assistance
Program at the Nebraska Medical Center in
Omaha, NE 68198

ABOUT THE BOOK

The Gutless Wonder is a true story of a young man faced with terrific pressures from secrets about his family. He kept this within himself and sought out the venue of playing high school football. His determination and will to never quit made it possible for him to achieve success under great physical and mental barriers that could not be understood by most everyone around him. His tragedies and accomplishments are detailed in the story and would give others a path to imitate if faced with similar situations.

ABOUT THE AUTHOR

Tom Rooney was chosen to tell his story of triumph over tragedy in order to keep the main character and others in the story anonymous. Also, the names of places have been changed, but the events, experiences, and memories have all been recorded to the best of the author's recollections. An effort was made not to embellish facts but to create a feeling for the burdens that Tom Rooney carried with him throughout his story. If this book will help just one individual through the tough times they may have to face in their teenage years, it has been worth all the effort.

CPSIA information can be obtained
at www.ICGtesting.com
Printed in the USA
LVHW112318100422
715847LV00016B/247